MARGARET LAURENCE

Born in Nccpawa, Manitoba, and educated at the University of Manitoba, Margaret Laurence has lived in England, Somaliland, and Ghana. She is best known for THE STONE ANGEL, A JEST OF GOD (which became the movie *Rachel, Rachel*) and THE DIVINERS, hallmarks of a career that have won her great popularity among readers and the highest praise from literary circles.

HEART OF A STRANGER

Now her legions of avid readers are offered a new perspective on Margaret Laurence, the sources of her art, her adventurous travels. For those not familiar with her fiction, here is a sparkling introduction to one of Canada's major authors.

Heart of a Stranger

Margaret Laurence

SEAL BOOKS
McClelland and Stewart-Bantam Limited
Toronto

HEART OF A STRANGER
*A Seal Book / published by arrangement with
McClelland and Stewart Limited*

PRINTING HISTORY
*McClelland and Stewart edition published September 1976
A Literary Guild selection Fall 1976
Seal edition / May 1980*

*Lines from "Roblin Mills Circa 1842" by Al Purdy
reprinted with permission of McClelland and Stewart Limited.
Lines from "On Completing a Life of Gabriel Dumont" by
George Woodcock reprinted with permission of the author.*

ISBN 0-7704-1582-2

*Seal Books are published by McClelland and Stewart-Bantam
Limited. Its trademark, consisting of the words "Seal Books"
and the portrayal of a seal, is the property of McClelland and
Stewart-Bantam Limited, 25 Hollinger Road, Toronto, Ontario
M4B 3G2. This trademark has been duly registered in the Trademarks Office of Canada. The trademark, consisting of the word
"Bantam" and the portrayal of a bantam, is the property of and
is used with the consent of Bantam Books, Inc. 666 Fifth Avenue, New York, New York 10019. This trademark has been duly
registered in the Trademarks Office of Canada and elsewhere.*

COVER PRINTED IN THE UNITED STATES OF AMERICA
TEXT PRINTED IN CANADA

Contents

"Also, thou shalt not oppress a stranger:
for ye know the heart of a stranger,
seeing ye were strangers in the land of Egypt."

EXODUS 23:9

Foreword

That verse from Exodus has always meant a great deal to me. I have spent a good many years of my adult life as a stranger in strange lands, in some cases as a resident, and in others as a traveller. I have met suspicion and mistrust at times, and I have also met with warmth and generosity. The process of trying to understand people of another culture—their concepts, their customs, their life-view—is a fascinating and complex one, sometimes frustrating, never easy, but in the long run enormously rewarding. One thing I learned, however, was that my experience of other countries probably taught me more about myself and even my own land than it did about anything else. Living away from home gives a new perspective on home. I began to write out of my own background only after I had lived some years away, and when I finally came back to Canada to stay, nearly ten years after I had returned in my fiction, I knew for certain that it was where I belonged, and I knew why.

And yet, for a writer of fiction, part of the heart remains that of a stranger, for what we are trying to do is to understand those others who are our fictional characters, somehow to gain entrance to their minds and feelings, to respect them for themselves as human individuals, and to portray them as truly as we can. The whole process of fiction is a mysterious one, and a writer, however experienced, remains in some ways a perpetual amateur, or perhaps a perpetual traveller, an explorer of those inner territories, those strange lands of the heart and spirit.

These articles and essays are very much interwoven with that process and with my own life. They were written between 1964 and 1975, and most of them were published in various places during that time. Some of them describe journeys in lands strange to me, and yet I believe they describe something of the inner journeys as well. Many also deal with themes that I dealt with later in my fiction. Although I did not fully realize it at the time, in a sense I was working out these themes in a non-fiction way before I found myself ready to deal with them in the broader form of the novel. I see them as travels and entertainments, but they are also a record of the long journey back home.

Margaret Laurence
Lakefield, Ontario
1976

Written in 1970, this article deals both with my debt to African writers and with my concepts of a writer's sources. I had not yet begun writing *The Diviners*, but it was very much in my mind and I was soon to begin it. The lines quoted here from one of Al Purdy's poems were the same lines I later quoted at the beginning of the novel. A rather curious aspect of this article is that it deals with the theme of survival. At that time, Margaret Atwood's *Survival* had not yet been written, and when she was writing her thematic study of Canadian literature, she had not read this article.

A Place to Stand On

"The creative writer perceives his own world once and for all in childhood and adolescence, and his whole career is an effort to illustrate his private world in terms of the great public world we all share."

Graham Greene, *Collected Essays*

I believe that Graham Greene is right in this statement. It does not mean that the individual does not change after adolescence. On the contrary, it underlines the necessity for change. For the writer, one way of discovering oneself, of changing from the patterns of childhood and adolescence to those of adulthood, is through the explorations inherent in the writing itself. In the case of a great many writers, this explanation at some point—and perhaps at all points—involves an attempt to understand one's background and one's past, sometimes even a more distant past which one has not personally experienced.

This sort of exploration can be clearly seen in the

1

works of contemporary African writers, many of whom re-create their people's past in novels and plays in order to recover a sense of themselves, an identity and a feeling of value from which they were separated by two or three generations of colonialism and missionizing. They have found it necessary, in other words, to come to terms with their ancestors and their gods in order to be able to accept the past and be at peace with the dead, without being stifled or threatened by their past.

Oddly enough, it was only several years ago, when I began doing some research into contemporary Nigerian writing and its background, that I began to see how much my own writing had followed the same pattern—the attempt to assimilate the past, partly in order to be freed from it, partly in order to try to understand myself and perhaps others of my generation, through seeing where we had come from.

I was fortunate in going to Africa when I did—in my early twenties—because for some years I was so fascinated by the African scene that I was prevented from writing an autobiographical first novel. I don't say there is anything wrong in autobiographical novels, but it would not have been the right thing for me— my view of the prairie town from which I had come was still too prejudiced and distorted by closeness. I had to get farther away from it before I could begin to see it. Also, as it turned out ultimately, the kind of novel which I can best handle is one in which the fictional characters are very definitely *themselves*, not me, the kind of novel in which I can feel a deep sense of connection with the main character without a total identification which for me would prevent a necessary distancing.

I always knew that one day I would have to stop writing about Africa and go back to my own people, my own place of belonging, but when I began to do this, I was extremely nervous about the outcome. I did not consciously choose any particular time in history, or any particular characters. The reverse seemed to be true. The character of Hagar in *The Stone Angel* seemed almost to choose me. Later, though, I recognized that in some way not at all consciously understood by me at the time I had had to begin approaching my background and my past through my grandparents' generation, the generation of pioneers of Scots-Presbyterian origin, who had been among the first to people the town I called Manawaka. This was where my own roots began. Other past generations of my father's family had lived in Scotland, but for me, my people's real past—my own real past—was not connected except distantly with Scotland; indeed, this was true for Hagar as well, for she was born in Manawaka.

The name Manawaka is an invented one, but it had been in my mind since I was about seventeen or eighteen, when I first began to think about writing something set in a prairie town. Manawaka is not my hometown of Neepawa—it has elements of Neepawa, especially in some of the descriptions of places, such as the cemetery on the hill or the Wachakwa valley through which ran the small brown river which was the river of my childhood. In almost every way, however, Manawaka is not so much any one prairie town as an amalgam of many prairie towns. Most of all, I like to think, it is simply itself, a town of the mind, my own private world, as Graham Greene says, which one hopes will ultimately relate to the outer world which we all share.

When one thinks of the influence of a place on one's writing, two aspects come to mind. First, the physical presence of the place itself—its geography, its appearance. Second, the people. For me, the second aspect of environment is the most important, although in everything I have written which is set in Canada, whether or not actually set in Manitoba, somewhere some of my memories of the physical appearance of the prairies come in. I had, as a child and as an adolescent, ambiguous feelings about the prairies. I still have them, although they no longer bother me. I wanted then to get out of the small town and go far away, and yet I felt the protectiveness of that atmosphere, too. I felt the loneliness and the isolation of the land itself, and yet I always considered southern Manitoba to be very beautiful, and I still do. I doubt if I will ever live there again, but those poplar bluffs and the blackness of that soil and the way in which the sky is open from one side of the horizon to the other—these are things I will carry inside my skull for as long as I live, with the vividness of recall that only our first home can have for us.

Nevertheless, the people were more important than the place. Hagar in *The Stone Angel* was not drawn from life, but she incorporates many of the qualities of my grandparents' generation. Her speech is their speech, and her gods their gods. I think I never recognized until I wrote that novel just how mixed my own feelings were towards that whole generation of pioneers—how difficult they were to live with, how authoritarian, how unbending, how afraid to show love, many of them, and how willing to show anger.

And yet, they had inhabited a wilderness and made it fruitful. They were, in the end, great survivors, and for that I love and value them.

The final exploration of this aspect of my background came when I wrote—over the past six or seven years—*A Bird in the House*, a number of short stories set in Manawaka and based upon my childhood and my childhood family, the only semi-autobiographical fiction I have ever written. I did not realize until I had finished the final story in the series how much all these stories are dominated by the figure of my maternal grandfather, who came of Irish Protestant stock. Perhaps it was through writing these stories that I finally came to see my grandfather not only as the repressive authoritarian figure from my childhood, but also as a boy who had to leave school in Ontario when he was about twelve, after his father's death, and who as a young man went to Manitoba by sternwheeler and walked the fifty miles from Winnipeg to Portage la Prairie, where he settled for some years before moving to Neepawa. He was a very hard man in many ways, but he had had a very hard life. I don't think I knew any of this, really knew it, until I had finished those stories. I don't think I ever knew, either, until that moment how much I owed to him. One sentence, near the end of the final story, may show what I mean. "I had feared and fought the old man, yet he proclaimed himself in my veins."

My writing, then, has been my own attempt to come to terms with the past. I see this process as the gradual one of freeing oneself from the stultifying aspect of the past, while at the same time beginning to see its true value—which, in the case of my own people (by which I mean the total community, not just my particular family), was a determination to survive against whatever odds.

The theme of survival—not just physical survival, but the preservation of some human dignity and in the end some human warmth and ability to reach out and touch others—this is, I have come to think, an almost inevitable theme for a writer such as I, who came from a Scots-Irish background of stern values and hard work and puritanism, and who grew up during the drought and depression of the thirties and then the war.

This theme runs through two of my novels other than *The Stone Angel* (in which it is, of course, the dominant theme). In *A Jest of God* and *The Fire-Dwellers*, both Rachel and Stacey are in their very different ways threatened by the past and by the various inadequacies each feels in herself. In the end, and again in their very different ways and out of their very different dilemmas, each finds within herself an ability to survive—not just to go on living, but to change and to move into new areas of life. Neither book is optimistic. Optimism in this world seems impossible to me. But in each novel there is some hope, and that is a different thing entirely.

If Graham Greene is right—as I think he is—in his belief that a writer's career is "an effort to illustrate his private world in terms of the great public world we all share," then I think it is understandable that so much of my writing relates to the kind of prairie town in which I was born and in which I first began to be aware of myself. Writing, for me, has to be set firmly in some soil, some place, some outer and inner territory which might be described in anthropological terms as "cultural background." But I do not believe that this kind of writing needs therefore to be parochial. If Hagar in *The Stone Angel* has any meaning, it is the same as that of an old woman anywhere, having to deal with the reality of dying. On the other hand, she is not an old woman anywhere. She is very much a person who belongs in the same kind of prairie Scots-Presbyterian background as I do, and it was, of course, people like Hagar who created that background, with all its flaws and its strengths. In a poem entitled *Roblin Mills, Circa 1842*, Al Purdy said:

> They had their being once
> and left a place to stand on

They did indeed, and this is the place we are standing on, for better and for worse.

I remember saying once, three or four years ago, that I felt I had written myself out of that prairie town. I know better now. My future writing may not be set in that town—and indeed, my novel, *The Fire-Dwellers*, was set in Vancouver. I may not always write fiction set in Canada. But somewhere, perhaps in the memories of some characters, Manawaka will probably always be there, simply because whatever I am was shaped and formed in that sort of place, and my way of seeing, however much it may have changed over the years, remains in some enduring way that of a small-town prairie person.

This article describes my first trip to Greece. It seems somewhat less ecstatic than might be expected from one's first sight of that ancient land, and I can only suppose that was because I had so seldom been a tourist and found the role a difficult one at first. In East and then West Africa, where we had lived a total of seven years, we had been outsiders, strangers, but not tourists.

⚭

Sayonara, Agamemnon

"Why be half-classical," my husband remarked, as we flicked through dozens of multi-tinted brochures in our Athens hotel room, "when the chance may never come again to be *ultra*-classical?"

So it was that we chose the Four Day Ultra Classical Tour. A tourist is not merely any traveller in a land unknown to him or her. A tourist, strictly speaking, is one who goes on tours. We have lived in England, Somaliland, and Ghana. We had visited various places in Italy and in India. Once, in England, we had won a modest amount in the football pools and had spent it all on a trip to Paris. We had travelled most of Canada. But we had never gone on a tour. For us, the Four Day Ultra Classical was a *rite de passage*, an initiation into the world of genuine tourism.

The portly man at the front of the bus seemed to be having some difficulty with the microphone. He blew delicately into it, and then whistled portions of what may have been the Greek national anthem, but the mechanism remained unresponsive. He sighed from his depths, and all at once the sound reverberated through the bus like the exasperation of a giant. The stout man beamed and bowed.

"Ladies and gentlemen, I bid you good morning." His voice rolled richly if a little tiredly around the old-fashioned phraseology, but there was some promising undertone of laughter as well. "I hope you will enjoy our tour of Delphi and the Peloponnesian peninsula. I will now introduce myself. My name is Nick."

I did not, of course, believe him. I thought he had been reading Damon Runyon and had decided to adopt this name for the sake of North Americans who believed all Greeks were called Nick. We discovered later that his name really was Nicholas, for he showed us a guidebook he had written. It was drably entitled *A Walk Through Athens*, and the writing was formal and stilted, the way he talked when he began that day. This style was the exact opposite of the way he spoke once he got going. When he became hooked by his subject, he would talk with fire, violently partisan, as though the wars between Athens and Sparta continued to the present time. Perhaps he was right. Seen as the struggle between the forces of growth and open inquiry, and those of fear and stultified thought, undoubtedly Athens and Sparta will always grapple for the souls of men.

Nick was very careful of how much he said, however, for the great danger was not in offending his audience but in boring them. His role as guide was a tricky one, for he had to appear to be an instructor when in fact he was being paid to be an entertainer. There must never be too long an interval between jokes. This performance was made considerably easier by some old-trouper quality in him, evident when he blossomed expansively at applauding laughter. He delivered his orations in English, French, and German, and he did the Four Day Ultra Classical twice a week. His week, he explained, had eight days. Actually, his routine throughout the summer was one tour, one day off, and then another tour. In the winter he painted watercolours of ruined temples, which his wife sold to the January foreigners, who didn't like to consider themselves tourists.

Our co-travellers could scarcely have been more varied. Mr. and Mrs. Webster were elderly Americans. He was a retired department-store executive who looked rather like Henry Miller in a beret. She, in sensible shoes and a manner of placid friendliness, carried an imposing first-aid kit and dispensed aspirin and milk-of-magnesia tablets to the needy among us. She was not all that strong and often got tired, but she never let on.

Herr and Frau Beck were Swiss. He was a surveyor, a man built like a bulldozer, with a thick neck and forward-thrusting shoulders. It must have been his thwarted ambition to be a clown, for he appointed himself tour comedian and worked diligently at the job. He had the most loyal wife I have ever seen. She was his cheering section. Whatever he said, her response was always an ebullient *"Jah!"*

Monsieur and Madame Lapointe were the antithesis of anyone's general notion of the French. Smart and sleek? The Lapointes were subdued as a mousy aunt and uncle. Voluble? The Lapointes barely opened their mouths. They were morose and reticent. They spoke one or two words of English, but our own national peculiarities came into effect here. Being Canadians of the English-speaking variety, we were so intensely mortified by our inability to speak French that we could not bring ourselves to speak to the Lapointes at all, not once in four days.

Mr. and Mrs. Takamura, from Tokyo, looked too young to have a grown-up daughter, but there she was, eighteen or nineteen, attractive in her sheath dress. It was Mrs. Takamura, however, who drew everyone's eyes wherever we went. She was slender but with no look of fragility, and she was immaculately dressed in a kimono. In the daytime it was silver-gray of a stiff crisp material that looked heavy, though she herself always looked cool, no matter how scorching the sun. In the evenings, for dinner, she put on a more elaborate brocade kimono, beige-gold, embroidered with waving grasses and small birds.

The bus winged along like a swallow over the Athenian plains, dry and hot as a desert. On either side of the road the pale, ripening wheat was stippled with the scarlet of poppies. Our ease and speed made a disquieting contrast to the local farmers' way of travel, which was by donkey. Donkeys everywhere, small and humble-looking, necks eternally bent. And roadside shrines, icons and a candle, sometimes flowers.

These roads, Mrs. Webster declared, were heaven after Africa, where she and her husband had spent the past three months at vast expense and in acute discomfort. Leroy did not mind the discomfort one scrap, she said admiringly. For thirty years he had been mad to see Africa, and now thank goodness he had seen it. They used to get up long before dawn, to go and sit beside some water-hole so Leroy could get pictures of bush buffalo.

Herr Beck decided to liven the drooping company.

He began to bray like a donkey. *Ee-aw! Ee-aw!* The noise charmed and hypnotized him. His wife laughed uproariously.

Then we were in the hills. Mr. Webster stopped the bus, declaring that Mount Parnassus would make a terrific picture.

"Come on, camera fans," he croaked in his cheerful frog-voice. "All out!"

And we obeyed, instantly converted by his eagerness into camera fans.

At Delphi, the scattered bones of the once-ornate temples could be imbued with life only if you happened to know much more about ancient Greece than I did. But the spring where the oracle priestess had ritually bathed—that conveyed something. It must have been splendid once, when the pool was tiled with white marble and decorated with elaborate carvings and flowers and ornaments of gold. Above and around it, the ravine stretched up, a fissure in the mountain, the stone coarse and rust-coloured, the trees wiry and oddly shaped.

Very young girls were chosen as oracles, Nick explained—girls who were not only beautiful but also pliant and agreeable to the guidance of the priests. The oracle act was not astonishing, he maintained with jovial scepticism. The priests had a mighty network of spies, so they were very well informed about matters of war and politics, and would tell the priestess what answer she was to give. If the priests were in doubt, they devised a mysterious answer that could be interpreted any way at all. Then, if disaster occurred after someone had taken the oracle's advice, the priests could always slither out of any blame by saying that the oracle had been misunderstood by the cloddish client.

"Priests can be quite talented in these ways," Nick said blandly.

He spoke as though the past and present were one, as though the priests were still the same priests, and as though the old gods were with us yet. He never said, "Zeus was the father of the gods." He always said, "Zeus *is* the father . . . " Whoever might slay Zeus, it would certainly not be Nick. But whether this apparent caution betokened a belief in all gods or a belief in none, I do not know.

Personally, I imagined an oracle of Delphi as similar to those fey girls who were said to attract poltergeists to houses, perhaps rather dull and even bovine on the surface, but capable of falling into an uncontrived trance. Surely, for a convincing performance, the young priestess must have had complete belief herself. She must have been fantastically nervous the first time, or maybe each time, as she was being garbed in various splendours, wondering if she could walk without stumbling all the long way to the temple and into the darkened room where the god, unheard by her, would speak through her voice.

Around the broken cream-coloured columns of the main temple we paced and peered. Suddenly a young man, leaping from nowhere like a mountain goat, capered around us with a camera, in absolute silence. He seemed like one of those mad seers or idiot shepherds who were always descending on the city in Greek plays and telling people things about themselves, usually of an exceedingly unpleasant nature. It turned out, however, that he was only a commercial photog-

13

rapher. He developed his films by some lightning process and offered them to us hopefully as we sat in a nearby café resting our feet.

"I have had my picture taken as many times as General de Gaulle," Nick declared.

Mr. Webster, exhausted and perspiring, discovered with delight that the café sold ice cream. He unslung his camera and settled down to a large vanilla cone.

"One thing you've got to admit," he said. "The ancient Greeks didn't have ice cream."

Nick put down his beer glass and drew himself up with ponderous dignity.

"Sir," he replied, "the ancient Greeks didn't *need* ice cream."

At night the village of Delphi was as quiet as though it had been utterly deserted. The stars were white, like floating petals in the deep pool of sky. A dog howled, and the sound was eerie against the hills. I wondered what a priestess of Delphi did when she grew old. Did she run a finishing school for aspiring oracles? Did she marry wealth and retire as a suburban matron? Did she die of poison administered by priests who thought she knew too much? Or did she simply leave the gaudy presence of the temples and move up into the mountains alone, to try to understand why the armies clashed so meaninglessly? But would an ex-oracle be permitted privacy? They probably discussed her at Athenian cocktail parties. "You really must get an audience with the Delphic oracle, darling. No, not that dim-witted girl they've installed in the temple. I mean the old one who's just retired. She knows simply everything about everybody. Her prophesies are too marvellous, and half the price."

By boat to Patras. In the ship's canteen, I bought

14

Rose-Flower-Leaf jam, which the label said was made from flowers gathered in monastery gardens and was very good for stomach ailments. Alas—as I might have guessed—it tasted like sugared perfume.

Another touring group, mainly Germans, was aboard. They remained close to us from this point onward, and we began to think of them as The Rivals, for they stayed at the same hotels as we did, and whoever got there first was given the best rooms. Nick settled down in conversation with his opposite number in the other tour, a determined lady who clutched a weighty text entitled *Griechenland*. Obviously the fact-loving members of her party weren't going to get the better of her.

Mr. and Mrs. Webster told us of their travels. They had been everywhere. Once in Egypt, when they were doing the Valley of the Kings, they had the misfortune to get a ninety-two-year-old alcoholic guide. "He had bottles stashed away in every corner of the tombs," Mrs. Webster recalled. "Leroy complained, and the next day we got a different guide. But they had decided to gang up on us. We got the old man's grandson, and he was in magnificent physical condition. We went at a killing pace, I'm telling you. The average number of tombs to see in a day is three. That day we saw well over two dozen tombs. We were dead beat, and Leroy got worried about me. Finally he said he thought we better quit. But I wouldn't. I just would not. 'No sir, Leroy,' I said, 'we're not giving up now. This is a matter of national honour.' "

I warmed to them enormously, seeing them tottering through tomb after tomb, gritting their teeth, getting bunions for the honour of their country.

A young American couple sat edgily on deck chairs

beside us, keeping a nervous eye on their children, who were spinning around the boat like two gusts of wind. Finally the mother could stand it no longer. They absolutely had to sit down, she decreed, and quit leaning over the railing before she went out of her mind entirely. Dejectedly they sat, and were immediately seized with total boredom. What, they enquired shrilly, was there to *do*? The Takamuras' daughter picked up an old newspaper and went to sit beside the children. Effortlessly, she folded the paper into wonderful shapes—birds and fishes, stars and lanterns. The two whirlwinds spent the rest of the voyage mercifully and quietly enchanted. When we docked at Patras, they followed their parents off the boat and turned to wave goodbye. "*Sayonara*," they called, preening at their mastery of what may very well have been the only foreign word they learned in Greece. "*Sayonara!*"

At Patras we walked down to the harbour after lunch. To our amazement, one of the ships docked there was called *Hesperus*. Herr and Frau Beck looked bewildered, unable to see the reason for our laughter. Herr Beck looked at his watch and realized it was time to return to the bus, which had accompanied us on the boat to Patras.

"*Komm*," he said, a short sharp bark of command. His wife wheeled instantly, as though radio-controlled, and trotted along after him.

Mrs. Webster, strolling, stared in disbelief.

"Golly," she said. "Get a load of that, will you? She laughs like crazy at every single one of his jokes, too. How different from us—old sourpuss me, anyway."

In the drowsy afternoon and the soporific humming of the bus, even Nick dozed. Only Herr Beck felt that he had not come on a tour in order to sleep. Music and action were what he craved. He did his animal imitations first, and the donkey bray effectively wakened everyone. He could also crow like a rooster, we learned. His wife chortled with unaffected enjoyment. Next he began to sing "Tannenbaum," and went on to an assortment of ballads that grew progressively more tearful and emotional.

"He'll be singing 'Lili Marlene' next," Mrs. Webster muttered.

Gray-green olive trees flashed by, and massive bushes of pink oleander. In villages, red geraniums grew at every doorstep. People did not bother to look up as we passed, for the tour buses zoomed along here every few minutes. The bus seemed like a time machine in a science-fiction story, a vehicle permitting one to glimpse but not to touch the visited centuries. Inside our metal-and-glass bubble, Herr Beck began to sing "Lili Marlene."

Olympia, the birthplace of the Olympic games. Gentle hills, and olive trees standing low and soft-coloured beside dark cypress shaped like spearheads. At the hotel, The Rivals' bus had arrived before us, so Nick was gloomy. Herr Beck greeted the German tourists warmly, especially two handsome girls with whom he linked arms and sang jolly songs, while Frau Beck beamed.

At the stadium there is an arch through which the athletes used to go on their way into the arena—men brawny as bison, almost too perfectly muscled and matted with oil. They must have plastered the oil on pretty thickly, for they had to scrape it off with special blades afterwards, Nick had informed us as he pointed out these bizarre instruments in the museum.

17

"If only that kid would get out of the way," Jack said, "I'd take a picture of the arch."

I suggested that he take a picture anyway, with the denim-clad American boy walking into the ancient stadium—Today facing Yesterday. He agreed and prepared to take his picture. At that precise moment the boy turned around. Today was facing Today, and they were both holding cameras aimed at each other.

Toward the ancient Romans, Nick felt only scorn and loathing. He never permitted us to look at the Roman section of any museum. Debased sculpture, he would say, and hurry us on. At the stadium in Olympia, he explained in detail how the games had deteriorated under the Roman rule. No standards any more. Everything went to pieces. The Emperor Nero even participated in the chariot race on one occasion. Nero, being no athlete, toppled out of his chariot. The race stopped. Two officials picked up Nero, dusted him off, and replaced him. The race resumed. Once more the emperor fell out. Once more the race stopped until the boss was hefted back into his chariot. And so it went. But when the race was ended, guess who was declared the winner. Nick heaved a mammoth sigh. That was the Romans for you.

Mrs. Webster, in the meantime, had been resting her feet and thinking her own thoughts.

"Who did you say?" she enquired, when the pantomime was over.

Nero, Nick told her, the Emperor Nero. Mrs. Webster smiled gently in recognition.

"Oh yes, him," she said. "He was a pill."

So much for Nero, who burned Christians like candles. The Lapointes were wandering shyly, touching the stone columns. Herr Beck tried out the valley to see if yodelling would carry. It did. Mrs. Takamura took a picture of her husband posing in the stadium as a discus thrower. They then walked appealingly hand in hand until we returned to the bus, when Mr. Takamura was unexpectedly overcome with the athletic spirit of the place. In a swiftly mettlesome burst of exuberance, he raced the bus back to the hotel, and—to everyone's relief—won.

In the morning we tumbled out at dawn and found The Rivals already in the lobby. Nick was eyeing them irritably, assessing their readiness for the takeoff, and pacing with impatience as he waited for us.

"*Auf wiedersehen!*" Herr Beck bellowed to the German girls, as we scurried towards our respective buses for the next lap of the race.

The fortress at Mystras, near the place where ancient Sparta used to stand, was begun by returning Crusaders and ultimately spread all over the mountain.

"I am descended," Nick said, striking an attitude of caricatured nobility, "from the originator of this fortress. Anyway, we have the same name, so who knows?"

Once there were 130 churches here. This number stuck in my mind, because I imagined that there could not have been much room left for houses. We entered several of these dank Byzantine churches, which I found morbid and yet fascinating. There was a terrible sense of being enclosed, of some desperate attempt to shut out a threatening world. But the pain in the faces of the paintings seemed to indicate that the inner world had been just as threatening. One church was still in use. Red and white lilies smelled decayingly sweet beside the altar, and nearby hung a thousand small metal portrayals of sick limbs, sick eyes, sick

children. The painting above these votive offerings
was grotesque—a saint with drawn silver sword and
an open lovely face, and on his belly the same face
fallen into absolute corruption, a Byzantine Dorian
Gray.

Relieved to be back in the fresh air, we stumbled
down the mountain for lunch under the orange trees.
But The Rivals had beaten us, so we had to wait. Mrs.
Webster passed the time by telling me exotic medical
facts. There is this disease of the inner ear that strikes
when people (especially women) are allergic to alco-
hol. Your ears ring, you become faint and sometimes
you even fall down. No, no, Mrs. Webster said, the
condition is not to be confused with inebriation. The
test for this ailment is very interesting. The doctor
and his nurse each take a syringe and squirt a jet of
cold water into your ears simultaneously. If you can
then stand up, you haven't got it.

I said that I could not imagine anyone standing up,
ever again.

"It's all a question of your equilibrium," Mrs. Webster said.

Nauplia and the Bay of Argolis. It would have been
pleasant to be able to think, *fabled Argolis, from
whence sailed So-and-So on his way to Somewhere-or-
Other*. But nothing was certain to me. History and
legend shimmered like mirages, distant and unclear,
though we were on closer ground with the grim fortress at Nauplia, which had been built, Nick said, by
the Venetians.

"Great sailors, the Phoenicians," Mr. Webster commented, being slightly hard of hearing, especially on
heights and in the wind. "World's first traders. Sailed
all over, the Phoenicians did—you know that?"

At the hotel, a minor victory. We beat The Rivals and therefore got the seafront rooms. That evening, our last of the tour, the Websters gave a party. Communications were difficult. The Websters, the Takamura family, and ourselves spoke English, but otherwise nobody could speak to anyone else, except for Nick, who could speak to everybody. The burden of social discourse fell entirely upon him. He kept things going by telling jokes in three languages. All his jokes were about drunken Greeks. In one of them, two men were holding an argument about whether the light in the sky was the sun or the moon, so they asked a passerby to give his opinion. He replied, "I really can't say—I'm a stranger here myself." Nick was like a conductor, and we were the sections of his orchestra, each section waiting its turn. The laughter came in small separate waves.

On the final day we saw Mycenae, and I felt at last the actuality of the past, the certainty that the characters had been flesh and breath, and it had not been so very long ago. The stones of Mycenae are huge and rough. This is the citadel of a people who were still half barbaric. At the Lion Gate the stone roadway is deeply grooved where the wheels wore it away, among them the wheels of Agamemnon's chariot returning from Troy.

The air was dry and still, and the insects whirred in the wild thyme on the hillside. All at once it became clear and recognizable—that moment in time when the air held the metallic clatter of those wheels on this stone, and when the watchman leaped from this hollowed-out alcove inside the walls and unbarred the heavy gates, and when the city shouted while Agamemnon, King of Men, mounted the winding road that led him to his palace and his death.

Nick, at the trench graves within the walls, was talking about the discoveries of Schliemann, the great German archaeologist, in his excavation at Mycenae. An absorbing subject and one that had long interested me, but this did not seem the moment for it. I wanted to climb by myself to the hilltop where the palace had once stood.

I reached the site of the palace. The stones were in disarray, and thorny bushes grew beside the fallen walls, but some outlines of rooms remained. It was easy to imagine the king, a warrior by skill and a warrior in his concepts, expecting a pleased pride from his queen. And her, terrified, but with the memory of the child burning at her, their youngest child whom the king had sacrificed to the gods for luck in war. Even as she greeted him, this memory had been compelling her towards the revenge that would have no ending, but would finally be turned against her as she died at the hands of her son.

All at once a slight scuffling sounded from behind the stone walls, and a face appeared.

"Hi," a small girl said in American.

The ghosts withdrew, and the day was now, and I had to laugh.

"Hi," I said, where Agamemnon fell.

Nick ushered us to see the beehive burial place that is known as Agamemnon's Tomb. It was lofty and black inside, and Nick carried a lighted candle. We crept around the tomb, commenting irreverently. Then, unexpectedly, Nick made an invocation.

"I call upon you, spirits of the dead kings. But if

you don't speak English, that is just too bad, because I cannot speak to you in Greek."

He then laughed quickly, in case anyone might get the idea that he meant a word of it. On the bus, he began to sing from *I Pagliacci*. After a moment he stopped, perhaps feeling that this wasn't exactly the way to express his mood either. But soon the stone citadel relinquished him, at least sufficiently for him to begin clicking once more with his audience, telling the old tales jauntily, and even enjoying the flutter of responding laughter.

The red poppies were streaked like newly spilled blood across the wheat fields. But the giant stones of Mycenae were diminishing in the distance. We drove on, back to Athens.

So—*Sayonara*, Agamemnon. Or, as Mr. Webster claims they say in his country, don't take any wooden nickels.

The initiation was over. We were qualified tourists.

This was the first article I ever had published. It appeared in 1964. I was nervous about it because the friend I was describing was still living in Ghana, a known opponent to the Nkrumah regime. I took pains to conceal his identity—his name isn't Mensah and he isn't a lawyer. He subsequently got out of Ghana, with his family, and lived in America for some years. After the fall of Nkrumah, he was able to return home.

❦

The Very Best Intentions

"Come in," Mensah said, making it sound like "Stay out."

The bungalow was small and whitewashed, overgrown with purple bougainvillaea and surrounded by pawpaw trees and giant clusters of canna lilies. The low wall around the garden gave the feeling of privacy, if not the reality. Outside, the streets buzzed and clanged with voices and bicycles, and the air was heavy with the rich cloying smell of plantains being fried in palm oil, as the trader women beside their roadside stalls blew and stirred at the red coals of their charcoal pots. This was Ghana, five years before Independence. We had come here to live because my husband, a civil engineer, was working on the new harbour at Tema, which would at last provide the capital city of Accra with an adequate port.

"Will you have tea?" Mensah enquired, waving us to chairs.

Mensah was a young barrister. We had friends in common in London, so we had decided to look him up. Now I wondered if we had not made a mistake.

24

"If you're busy—" I faltered, expecting and hoping that he would make the conventional response, "No, no, of course not—do stay—"

Instead he said, "Busy? Africans are never busy. Didn't you know? It is because we are such an indolent people."

As I protested, embarrassed, Mensah laughed. At the time I naively imagined that he took us to be sahib-type Europeans, and I was frantic to correct his wrong impression. Later, however—several years later —I came to see that what he really dreaded was an encounter with yet another set of white liberals who went around collecting African acquaintances as though they were rare postage stamps. And now, at this further distance, I am not at all sure that I was not doing precisely that.

Because I lived in Ghana for five years, I am often asked what Ghanaians are like. I am always tempted to reply that it depends upon which Ghanaian you mean. West Africans, in popular mythological terms, are easy-going, extroverted people who have a marvellous sense of rhythm and who can dance to *highlife* music like jazzed-up angels because it is simply in them, something to do with the genes, perhaps. Mensah was the antithesis of this stereotyped image. He was tense as strained wire, introspective, meticulously neat, quick and even abrupt in his movements, and he would have scorned to dance *highlife* even if the salvation of his soul had depended upon it.

How our acquaintance ever survived those first few thorny years, I do not know. In the days when I first met Mensah, I still wore my militant liberalism like a heart on my sleeve. He was one of the first well-educated Africans whom I had met, and I was anxious to impress upon him not only my sympathy with African independence but also my keen appreciation of various branches of African culture—African sculpture, African literature, African traditions and proverbs. Mensah, however, as it turned out, couldn't have cared less about the African culture of the past. Strangely enough, it took me some time to realize that this represented only his own point of view and that all Africans did not necessarily think the same way. Our initial conversations were ridiculous and also (to me, anyway) painful, because whatever I happened to say always seemed to be the wrong thing.

I showed him an ebony head I had bought from a Hausa trader.

"Look—isn't this terrific? It's wonderful to see that carving is still flourishing in West Africa."

Mensah laughed disdainfully. "That? It's trash. They grind them out by the thousands. Europeans like that sort of thing, I suppose."

Both of us were exaggerating, trying to make some planned effect. I still have that carved ebony head. Now it seems neither as gorgeous as I claimed nor as awful as he said.

Mensah often employed shock treatment in talk. Once when I was extolling African drumming, telling him about a Yam Festival we had attended, and how the chief's drummer had played the *Ntumpane*, the great talking drums, Mensah clenched his hands in a sudden angry gesture.

"I am not such an admirer of these things as you are. Listen—shall I tell you something? My grandfather decorated his drums with human skulls. You see?"

He did not say any more. But I stared at him, seeing for the first time how he must look at the ancient Africa, the Africa of the talking drums and the bizarre figures cast in bronze. I could afford to be fascinated. None of it threatened me. But for Mensah, the time to move on had not only arrived, it was long overdue. What he saw in the old Africa was not the weird beauty of wood carvings or bronze vessels or the exultant pulsing of the drums. What he saw was the fear and the squalor, the superstition, the men still working the fields in this century with machetes and hoes, the children who still died by the score through lack of medical care.

As a matter of fact, I think it is highly unlikely that Mensah's grandfather ever decorated his drums with skulls, this interesting custom having died out in that part of the world many years ago. But even when I knew him better I never asked him, because it did not matter. If it wasn't actually true, it was dramatic emphasis—and it made the point all right.

But Mensah's attitude towards the totality of the past was subtle and paradoxical. On the surface, he appeared to take one clear line—the rejection of everything that had gone before.

"African history?" he would say mockingly. "Africans have no history."

At first this view distressed me, because I thought he meant it, and I would speak well-meaningly of the books on the subject which I had read, imagining him to be unacquainted with them, and insisting that Africans *had* a history, a history as long and as complex as that of any other country. Mensah would smile satirically and let me go on talking. Then he would place the tips of his fingers together as though about to make some weighty pronouncement, a mannerism of his which seemed to have been carried over from the courtroom.

"No, no," he would say, with a soft vehemence. "We are a simple people, you see. We have sprung directly from the loins of earth. History is too complicated a concept for us."

I began to comprehend, a little, his anger—which was partly a kind of self-torture. He knew as much about African history as anyone, and yet it was true that a great deal of African history was lost, perhaps lost irretrievably or perhaps awaiting partial rediscovery by archaeologists. I think Mensah reproached himself bitterly for caring that so much had been lost. I also came to see this line of his as a form of gamesmanship aimed at my white liberalism. The possession of a history, after all, is like the recognition of another person's common humanity—if it cannot be taken for granted, it means you do not really believe in it at all. Mensah never actually said this, but it was there, implicit in his sardonic laughter.

Our mistrust of one another, and perhaps of ourselves as well, must have gone deep. For a long time I did not trust Mensah enough to disagree with him, for fear of damaging what I hoped was his impression of me—which was actually only my own impression of myself: sympathetic, humanitarian, enlightened. For his part, he did not trust me enough to permit himself ever to agree with me on any issue at all. Yet the force which made us seek each other's company must have been the sense we both had of being somehow out of tune with the respective societies in which we lived.

I was not only unwilling but also unable to act like a *memsahib*, even when politeness temporarily demanded it. Mensah was hypercritical of the Europeans ("these white men") who were still in positions of power, but at the same time he was unable to side entirely with any politician or statesman among his own countrymen, because he could never subdue his questioning approach toward everything. He was not much of a man for waving flags, but he was living at a time when flags were being waved mightily and anyone who did not take an enthusiastic part in this popular pastime might well feel out of step. Because he nagged away at all political parties, I told him the only solution would be for him to form his own.

"Yes," he said. "That would be a really effective political weapon, wouldn't it? A party of one."

Social occasions with Mensah were never smooth. When we invited him to our place he would invariably arrive about two hours late, and I would be trying to contain my own annoyance and to placate our Nigerian cook, who would be beside himself with rage over his ruined meal, and blowing off steam by making loud and insulting remarks about all Ghanaians. Whenever we were invited to Mensah's we would arrive on the dot, thus throwing Mensah into a frenzy of consternation over the unready dinner. To him it was exceedingly thoughtless, and even rude, for guests to arrive on time. After Mensah married, the situation eased. His wife Honour did the cooking herself because she wanted to, although this was not customary in the families of professional men. If we forgot and arrived on time, Honour would somehow contrive to hurry the dinner and our *gaffe* would not be too obvious.

Mensah's son was born about the same time as ours, and in the same hospital, so for a few months before and after the babies were born, I talked mainly to Honour when we met, since both of us were almost totally absorbed in the question of children. Honour's personality was the opposite of her husband's and this must have worked to their mutual advantage. Where Mensah was like a leopard, always pacing some invisible cage, Honour was placid and calm, very firm in her opinions but never heatedly so.

I used to envy Honour sometimes, for socially she had far more freedom than I. She never had to worry about leaving the baby in the care of someone sufficiently responsible; both grandmothers were temporarily in residence, and Honour could go out any time she liked. I mentioned this to her, and she smiled.

"Yes, it's wonderful in some ways," she said. "But can you imagine having two women telling you what you are doing wrong with the baby? And both of them with ideas of child care which you don't accept?"

Honour was much more outspoken than Mensah when it came to family matters.

"When you put our two families together, Mensah's and mine, it adds up to a lot of people, and they all have the feeling that because Mensah is a lawyer he must be tremendously wealthy. I tell you, it is not so easy."

When at last we both emerged from our preoccupation with the babies and rejoined the general conversation, I realized that some change had gradually taken place without anyone's being aware of it. I no longer agreed, out of some need for his acceptance, with nearly everything Mensah said, and he no longer disagreed with nearly everything I said. Perhaps we were both beginning to trust one another enough to say what we really thought. Or perhaps we had begun to exist for one another as individuals with names and families, people with specific interests and with viewpoints which were our own.

I asked Mensah once why he had decided to go into law.

"Very simple," he said. "You see, people here love litigation. With us, it is a form of entertainment. Whatever happens in this country, good times or bad, there will always be hundreds of cases being fought in court over a sack of yams that somebody's grandmother stole half a century ago. I thought—how can I lose? If I am a barrister, I am certain to make my fortune."

"And will you?"

"No," Mensah replied. "Too many of my contemporaries had the same idea."

I left Ghana just before Independence, when the entire country was in a state of frantic excitement. The bickering over the constitution had risen in the past year almost to the point of hysteria, and the province of Ashanti had threatened to secede from the union, but now the regional differences had been overcome, or at least shelved, in the interests of Independence *now*, not later.

"Free-Dom" was the chant of the big-hipped market women as they marched in the forefront of the political parades.

"Aren't you pleased?" I asked Mensah.

31

"I am pleased, yes, of course. But I would be even more pleased if I did not see quite such a large hotel being built by the government for visiting important personages. Well, Nkrumah is giving us circuses now. We will see if the bread comes later. At least he understands one thing that most of his faithful followers do not."

"What's that?"

"The real difficulties," Mensah said grimly, "have not yet begun."

I did not expect ever to see Mensah again after I left Ghana, but I did see him. He visited Canada one year, and we happened to be in the same city at the same time. I met him for a drink and he told me his reactions to my country.

"Canadians are so touchy. Why didn't you tell me? I never knew. I thought if you said *Americans*, that meant all North Americans. I was really in trouble here, at first."

I said that his experience was poetic justice, thinking of my own blunders in Africa, and with a grin Mensah conceded that this might be so.

He told me about Ghana. Europeans in senior posts had been replaced with Africans, which he felt was a good thing. Building had been going on rapidly. The harbour was now completed and in operation. In one sense, things were booming. But Mensah was intensely alarmed at the increasing concentration of power in the hands of one man.

"You've read about it in the newspapers, of course? Well, the reports are stupid—they speak as though Nkrumah were making himself into a European-style dictator. He's not. He's the African king-figure, the greatest of all paramount chiefs. That is the image he is trying to create. Very clever, but perhaps very dangerous also. The King—he who possesses supernatural powers. In the end, does this take us ahead—or where? Really, you know, he has accomplished a great deal in a short time. But I would feel happier if he were not so ambitious. He is called *Osagyefo* now —the Redeemer. What will bring him down, I think, is not anything within the country, but his aspirations to be the leader of pan-Africanism. That is pure fantasy."

Then Mensah laughed in the mocking way I remembered so well.

"What I really have to complain about," he said, "is that I can't listen to the radio any more. I miss that very much."

"Why can't you listen?"

"Well, you see, every second word is *Osagyefo—Osagyefo—Osagyefo*. I am afraid that I may possibly die of boredom, so I have to turn the radio off."

Mensah's Christmas cards always bore some kind of barbed comment. That year, his card showed a picture of the triumphal Independence Arch in Accra. Opposite the words "Freedom and Justice," which appeared in large letters along the top of the arch, Mensah had penned a small question mark.

After I came to live in England, I got a postcard one day. "Am visiting England briefly. Will be in London on my way back to Ghana." And there, a few days later, was Mensah, looking a little older, but as tense and alert as always. I had invited two other friends who had attended London University with Mensah some years ago. Mensah, to my astonishment, started in once more on the "Africans have no history" line. I watched, half amused and half infuriated, while our friends pointed out gently to Mensah that there were, after all, the Benin bronzes and the ruins of Zimbabwe. The next day Mensah came over by himself.

"You really played the old tune again last night, didn't you?" I said.

He grinned. "Don't you think it's interesting to observe the reactions?"

"Oh, certainly I think so—now that I'm not being observed."

"After a while people begin to understand," Mensah said, not smiling now, "that everyone has a history, just as everyone has a skin—life isn't possible without it. But the most important thing about it is that it isn't important."

I didn't agree with him on that point, but we didn't have long to talk. It does not seem to me that we talked about anything very significant. Yet maybe it was the most significant things of which we spoke—our families, our work, where each of us thought we were going in this life and where we wanted to go. We exchanged our news quite plainly, because by this time we had known each other for a dozen years, and what happened to each of us and to our respective children was somehow important to the other. There is a point at which, without anyone having done anything to bring it about, a friend becomes an old friend. This, in the Ghanaian phrase, is something life dashes you for nothing—a present, more than you expected.

Mensah spoke scathingly of the writeups on Ghana which had appeared in the world press.

"You know what the trouble is? They see what amounts to a one-party system, and without trying to understand it or see what has formed it, they condemn it outright. It is not that I am in favour of a one-party system. It is just that I think that the western countries look at Ghana and shake their heads very sorrowfully, simply because our development obviously is not going to mirror their own. It is like saying, 'Of course I acknowledge your right to be free, as long as you always do the same as I do.'"

And yet from his point of view, the situation in Ghana was not heartening. We discussed the dismissal of a high court judge. I asked Mensah if his own position as a lawyer was not a precarious one. He nodded. The choices did not appear to be many—stay and keep one's criticism to oneself, or else go, which was not such a simple matter, either. Honour and the children had to be considered. There was the sheer practical difficulty of getting permission to leave, and there was the other thing, the inner conviction that one must stay, at least as long as possible, and find some way to speak what one felt to be true. But there was no place at the moment, it seemed, for loyal opposition. That might come later on, but what about the meantime? Mensah, standing by the window, suddenly swung around.

"To tell you the truth," he said brusquely, and with a bleakness I had never heard in his voice before, "I really do not know what to do. Perhaps I will discover."

After he had returned to Ghana, I received a Christmas card from Mensah. On the front of the card was a picture of an African woman carrying a large black cooking-pot on her head. Opposite the cooking-pot was Mensah's neatly penned comment—"Culture." I liked this very much, because it was aimed at the thing he really despises more than anything else— phoniness, whether from African supernationalists or white liberals.

I was reminded of another of Mensah's cards. It seemed to me then that if Freedom and Justice ever had any actuality, in any country, there must always, surely, be someone there who would place beside the words his own individual question mark.

I wrote this essay for my own interest in 1964, just after the publication of *The Stone Angel*, when I could not yet get back to doing any fiction. I was somehow drawn to the figure of this early nationalist leader in Somaliland, and had the feeling that his life had something to tell me. I had become interested in Mahammed'Abdille Hasan when we lived in Somaliland, and he is referred to in my book, *The Prophet's Camel Bell*, although not at length, and without much of the material which I discovered from later reading. I put the article away and gave it no more thought for many years. It seems to me now a rather curious piece of work, because I was making some attempt not only to tell the Sayyid's story but also to understand the plight of a tribal people faced with imperialist opponents who do not possess superior values, but who have greater material resources and more efficient weapons of killing. A long time later, this same theme came into my novel, *The Diviners*, in the portions which deal with the Highland clans and with the prairie Métis. This essay has never been published before.

The Poem and the Spear

For twenty years he fought them. He fought their rifles with spears. Then he fought their Maxim guns with rifles. Only at last when their destruction came from the sky was he unable to go on fighting against the impossible odds he had set himself. For he was a desert chieftain in one of the poorest and most desolate areas on earth, and he was pitting himself against what was then the greatest imperialist power in the world. He was fighting for two things—his land and his religion. And throughout his lifetime of battling, he employed what must surely be the strangest of all military weapons—poetry.

To his followers, he was Sayyid, Noble Lord, follower of the Prophet. To the British he was the Mad Mullah, demented preacher of Islam. Mahammed 'Abdille Hasan of Somaliland was in fact an early nationalist leader whose vision outstripped the possibilities of the age in which he lived.

Yet in a sense that is still putting too facile an interpretation upon him. He himself remains hidden, as he did for so long to the British, who never once saw him in person. His life is patterned with paradox. The man evades any nets of neat phrases which might bind him. He slips away, still unknown, just as he and his Dervish horsemen slipped through the British lines so many times, so long ago.

Mahammed 'Abdille Hasan was born in 1864, in the bleak stretches of the Haud plateau, in the eastern part of what was to become the Somaliland Protectorate. His father belonged to the Ogaden tribe, and his mother was a Dolbahanta. The Somali tribal system is a complex one. In this region, there are two main tribal divisions, the Darod and the Isaaq, and within each there exist many different clans and sub-clans. Mahammed 'Abdille Hasan's tribal affiliations were all with the Darod, so it was inevitable that in his wars much of his support would be drawn from this section of the Somali people.

The Somalis are nomadic, most of them living by keeping herds of camels and sheep, and moving seasonally with their stock from the watering places to the grazing grounds. These treks often involve going for days without water, walking across the hard red soil of the Haud plains where the thorny acacia trees grow, and the giant spiked aloes with their outstretched cactus arms, and where in the drought of the *Jilal* season the bodies of camels dead from thirst are fed upon by the great black vultures. It is no wonder that the Somali tribesmen are hardy and enduring, for only the strong survive.

Mahammed 'Abdille Hasan must have been brought up, like most Somali children, to endure privation when necessary, to gorge on camel meat and milk when these were available, to give thanks to Allah for the gift of a day's life, to take early his share of the men's work, to know the footprints of his own camels in the sand, to become a skilled spearman and horseman, to be merciless to his enemies and unfailingly generous to those of his own blood, to keep the fast of Ramadan and to observe the hours of prayer, to seek honour where a man should find it—in battle and the loot of battle—and to accept the will of Allah, living or dying. The social code of the Somali tribes. The religious code of Islam. The harsh code of survival developed by those who dwell in deserts.

Unlike many Somali boys of the time, however, Mahammed 'Abdille Hasan received an education. He began studying the Qoran at the age of seven and could read The Book by the time he was ten. He left the life of a camel herder when he was fifteen and became a teacher of religion. At nineteen he won the title of Sheikh for his knowledge of Islamic theology and Arabic philosophy and literature. Somali was an unwritten language then, and although throughout his life Mahammed 'Abdille Hasan composed almost all his poems in Somali, his long vitriolic correspondence with the British was conducted in Arabic.

He left home when he was in his twenties and

travelled for a few years, visiting Ethiopia, Italian Somaliland, and the Sudan. About 1894 he went on the *Haj*, the pilgrimage to Mecca, and this proved to be the turning point in his life. While at Mecca, he encountered Sayyid Mahammed Saalih, who had founded a religious order, the Saalihiya, a strict and reformist sect of Islam, a kind of Muslim puritanism. Mahammed 'Abdille Hasan joined the Saalihiya. Their doctrines became a ruling force to him, so much so that years later, during his fight with the British, the war cry of his followers was *Mahammed Saalih!* One of the few poems which Mahammed 'Abdille Hasan composed in Arabic rather than Somali was a hymn to the founder of the Saalihiya, and this hymn was used as a rallying song for the Dervish forces. The style shows the influence of the Qoran in the long, flowing, emotional lines filled with superlatives.

Oh miraculous man of God, Sheikh Mahammed Saalih,
    the helper, Mahammed Saalih.
Oh my teacher, my refuge, my stay, my reliance!
You are the epitome, the essence of saints. . . .
My heart is torn apart by longing, oh suns of the
    beloved.
You are my soul, my breath, oh most compassionate
    of the compassionate.
You are the seal of the faithful, the path of the caliphs.
You are the helper of mankind and djinns. . . .
Oh say to the weariness of my ribs, 'I bring good news
    to the faithful.'

When Mahammed 'Abdille Hasan returned to Somaliland, he preached the doctrines of his order at Berbera. It was a semi-ascetic life he advocated. He was opposed to luxury of all kinds, to smoking and to the chewing of *qat*, a leaf with a stimulant effect.

He also preached against a Roman Catholic mission which in those days was stationed at Berbera, accusing them of converting Somali children to Christianity by bribing them with food. Famine is a common condition in Somaliland, and possibly the fathers of the mission were acting only out of the injunction to Feed My Lambs. That was not quite the way it looked to the parents of the Somali children, however. What they saw was what Mahammed 'Abdille Hasan saw—their children being drawn into the paths of the infidel and therefore doomed to damnation. Mahammed 'Abdille Hasan became so involved with this question that he ultimately came to believe that the aim of British colonization was the Christianizing of the Somalis. Whether or not he was right in this belief is not really the point. He felt keenly the sting of colonialism; his land and his people were being governed by outsiders, non-believers who permitted within this Islamic stronghold the presence of Christian proselytizers.

In 1897, Mahammed 'Abdille Hasan returned to the Dolbahanta, his mother's people, and preached among them. He seems at this time to have begun to realize that his words and his personality were capable of exerting a powerful influence over people. He began to hear various tribal disputes, to give judgements, and to settle quarrels. The British administration in Berbera heard of him for the first time in 1899 when the rumour reached them that a young sheikh in the Haud was gaining a considerable following and was said to be attempting to buy smuggled rifles.

In August of that year, Mahammed 'Abdille Hasan with five thousand men raided the small settlement of Burao. His followers, who called themselves Dervishes, were mostly armed with spears, although two hundred of them had rifles. Although they did not remain in Burao long, through this attack Mahammed 'Abdille Hasan had proclaimed the *Jihad*, the holy war. When his forces had withdrawn and returned to the Haud, he sent a letter to the British.

You have oppressed our ancient religion without cause. Whatever people obey you, they are liars and slanderers.

The British Consul-General at Berbera at once declared Mahammed 'Abdille Hasan a rebel. The long battle had begun.

That first token raid on Burao was followed by further raids on Isaaq tribes, and the British administration soon became alarmed. The situation was strangely precarious on both sides. In 1900, the British occupied only three coastal towns and a few small outposts in the interior, and in none of these places was their holding force a large one. Mahammed 'Abdille Hasan, who was roaming the Haud trying to muster support for his cause, was unquestionably dominant in the Ogaden country, along the Ethiopian border, but he was by no means certain of the unqualified support of even the Darod clans of his own blood. Most of the Isaaq sections of the Somali people, those who lived closer to the coast and were thus within the British sphere of influence, at this juncture opposed him. Nevertheless he took the title of Sayyid and declared his intention—to fight the British until he had forced them into the sea.

Sayyid is the title which was once given only to the direct descendants of the Prophet. It is still one of the highest titles in the Islamic world, but it has been extended to include any man who is truly a ruler, a king. The title was not given to Mahammed 'Abdille Hasan by the high officials of Islam. He appropriated it, and some years later he was to receive a rebuke from Mecca for having done so. Whether he began to call himself Sayyid, or whether his followers began to call him Sayyidi (my Lord), is not known. Perhaps it was in some way a merging of the two—he, ready to take the title as Caesar was ready; and they, eager to bestow it, not entirely for the sake of flattery, but also in order to believe their leader worthy of it and therefore able to be all-protecting. Despite his pride and presumption in assuming the name of Sayyid, Mahammed 'Abdille Hasan was not totally lacking in humour on the subject of titles. On one occasion a Somali messenger, bringing him a letter from the British Consul-General in Berbera, addressed him as Sayyidi.

"Carrying the words of the infidel, you yourself have become an infidel," he is said to have replied tartly. "Do not call me Sayyidi. You should call me Sahib."

The First Expedition against the Sayyid was begun by the British in 1901, under the command of Lieutenant Colonel Swayne. Mahammed 'Abdille Hasan was in the Haud with an estimated five thousand men. Only six hundred of these had rifles. The rest bore the traditional Somali weapon, the long spear. As allies, the British had the Ethiopians, who were moving in to the western edge of the Haud with fifteen thousand men. The British at this point believed the campaign against the Somali leader would not be a difficult one. Swayne's force, fifteen hundred Somalis with rifles, set off just after the rains. They met the Sayyid's forces and attacked. The British rifles, more than double the quantity possessed by the Dervishes, proved too strong for Mahammed 'Abdille Hasan, and he ordered a retreat. But Swayne's tribal levy could not stay in the Haud. They were cut off fifty miles from water, and were soon forced to return to Burao, the nearest wells.

Mahammed 'Abdille Hasan began a concentrated program of recruitment. He used every means he could find to enlist the uncommitted tribes to his cause—persuasion, threat, bribery. He had none of the modern means of propagandizing—no radio, no TV, not even the printed word. But he was a master of mass communication all the same. He kept among his close retinue a number of skilled reciters. Their duty was to memorize the poems composed by the Sayyid and then to go from tribe to tribe, chanting the *gabay* and teaching them to others. Thus the Dervish message—*our land and our religion*—spread from campfire to campfire across the Haud.

Among Somalis, the tradition of oral literature is an ancient one, and it is not unusual for a man to be able to commit to memory a great number of lengthy saga-like poems. In style, Somali poetry is formal and governed by strict rules, and the ordinary tribesmen form a critical and appreciative audience. There are numerous types of poetry, but the one which is most highly regarded and the most difficult to compose is the *gabay*, a long narrative poem, highly alliterative and containing many allusions to Islamic theology, Somali genealogy, history, and legend. Mahammed 'Abdille Hasan is said to have been one of the most talented *gabay*-makers in all Somali literature. His use of poetry throughout his campaigns, therefore, does not indicate that he composed trite propaganda pieces. His poems show a firm grasp of the intricacies of Somali literary style, and his own passionate beliefs give a strength and carrying power to the lines even in translation, although of course it is impossible to convey in translation the complexities and subtleties of the form as they occur in the original Somali.

In *The Path of Righteousness*, he set out to describe the good Muslim. This is a recruitment poem in which the Sayyid equated the devout with those who would follow him in the struggle against the English. Among the attributes of the true believer:

He who knows God and follows the Divine Law,
He who does not forget the faith which was set before him
And who does not deny it; the truth must be upheld.
He who fulfils the duties of charity and seeks what is perfect
And who does not break the fast; the month of Ramadan is holy.
And he who gives of his property and livestock with sincerity
And who makes no parade of his gifts.
He who does not scorn the origins and ways of the Somali
And who does not perform menial tasks for the wages of unbelievers.
He who devotes himself to the holy war and is garlanded with flowers.
He who turns against the English dogs
And who wins the victory and glory and the songs of praise.

In this poem Mahammed 'Abdille Hasan also indicated the way in which his thinking was developing politically and socially, for as one characteristic of the faithful man he lists "He who does not favour those to whom he is close in genealogical descent." This, from a man who had grown up within a closely integrated tribal system, seems remarkable for that time, when there could have been few men who looked beyond the immediate tribal loyalties. The poem ends with a statement of corporate responsibility—essentially an affirmation of the wider sense of tribe, the beginning of the sense of nationhood.

> He who answers all your needs,
> Who welcomes you like a kinsman in your day of
>   affliction,
> And who at the height of the drought does not bar
>   his gate against you—
> Is not he who never fails you in your weakness one of
>   the brethren?

In 1902 Swayne obtained a reinforcement of King's African Rifles, and moved against the Sayyid once more. At the same time, a remarkable Somali, Risaldar-Major Haji Musa Farah, led a detached Somali levy of 450 rifles a hundred miles across the waterless Haud, picking up some five thousand local tribesmen on his way, attacking the Dervish camps and capturing several thousand camels and sheep. This small triumph was a blow to the Sayyid, as his forces moved always with their families and depended on their livestock for meat and milk. Swayne did not fare as well as Haji Musa Farah. The Dervishes attacked at full strength, with horsemen and spearmen, and the contingent of King's African Rifles fell before them. The Somalis who had been persuaded into service on the British side began to doubt the wisdom of their choice.

Swayne, alarmed at the apparent demoralization of his supporting tribesmen, withdrew. This was the last time the British relied on tribal levies. Regular troops were to be used henceforth. An expedition was planned on a much larger scale, for the administration felt it was losing prestige. Mahammed 'Abdille Hasan would have to be defeated, and defeated quickly.

The Sayyid continued his attempts to win over more and more of the tribes. Sealing an alliance with the Majeerteen clan, he even made a present of his splendid horse, Hiin Finiin. He recorded in a *gabay* the personal cost of this gift. The affection he felt towards Hiin Finiin contrasts sharply with the vehemence of his feelings towards his enemies.

> . . . the beautiful one,
> He is bay, for in colour horses are not equal.
> Oh, the straight-limbed one; this beast is without peer,
> And whenever he comes into my thoughts, my love
>   for him is re-kindled.
> Nothing except the letter of my faith surpasses my
>   love for him.
> To mount him with might for the holy war was my
>   desire.
> On his back I would have claimed the rights of which
>   I was deprived;
> It was upon him that I intended to make a feast of
>   my enemies for the hornbill, witness of death.

Whatever the subject of Mahammed 'Abdille Hasan's poetry, the theme always returned to that of the central battle that had become his life's mission.

The British had many problems with the Third Expedition in 1903. Everything had to be transported out into the Haud by burden camels, and the difficulty of conveying enough water for men and animals was staggering. The force formed at Berbera, on the coast. They were a varied lot—Sikhs from India, Masai from Kenya, Sudanese, Boer troops from South Africa, an Ethiopian contingent, and Somalis from the coastal tribes.

Out they went into the broad empty stretches of the Haud, this unwieldy army, men and camels, horses and Maxim guns, across the sand where no roads existed, through matted underbrush of thorn bushes, over the plains where the grass in the good season after the rains grew as high as a horse's withers. No one knew where the Sayyid and his Dervishes were. A reconnaissance force was sent out to find him.

This smaller force camped at Gumburu. Before the night was over, the almost-tangible silence of the desert was splintered by the long wailing battlecry—*Mahammed Saalih!* The Dervish horsemen swept in, fighting with rifles and spears, attacking, withdrawing, bearing down again upon the men encamped behind their thornbough fence. The British had one Maxim gun, but it did not save them. The entire group was cut to pieces. Just before the Dervishes descended for the final time, Captain Johnston-Stewart broke up the Maxim gun so it could never be fired again. Bravery was not lacking, during these two decades of war, on either side.

The Sayyid's forces now established themselves in the Ogaden country, across the Ethiopian border. The ill-fated Third Expedition stayed for a time in the Haud, and there were some occasional skirmishes with the Sayyid's raiding parties. They could not, however, reach his main encampment without crossing more than a hundred miles of desert where there were no wells. This feat would have proved too much for the clumsy army, encumbered with heavy guns and ammunition, and hindered by lack of familiarity with the country. The Third Expedition took what small encouragement it could from the fact that they had Mahammed 'Abdille Hasan hemmed in. Even though they could not reach him, they felt, neither could he get out. It was stalemate, but not for long.

Unknown to the British, the Sayyid was planning a massive march back into British territory, to the Nogal Valley. The spring rains came with violence, the sky opening, a black flood of water cloaking the land, the storm winds screaming all through the nights, for no rain is as sudden and attacking as the desert rains. The Sayyid quickly took advantage of the natural turmoil and used it as his camouflage. In this incredible exodus, he took his entire fighting force, which could not have been less than five thousand of his most loyal warriors, as well as their families, wives, children, uncles and cousins, and all the countless thousands of camel, sheep and goats which were the necessary accompaniment to all his major treks. He moved them some two hundred miles, through the British lines. The first the British suspected of the operation was when they discovered that their telegraph lines had been cut. By then, however, Mahammed 'Abdille Hasan was ensconced in the strategically strong position of the Nogal Valley, where there were good wells and plentiful grazing and where the encampments, hedged with mountains, could not be attacked without warning. The letter which he sent to the British administration, after the Nogal march, was filled with his scathing irony and contained a reiteration of his goals.

We have fought for a year. I wish to rule my own country and protect my own religion. . . . If you wish, send me a letter saying whether there is to be peace or war. . . . We have both suffered considerably in battle. . . . God willing, I will take many rifles from you, but you will not get any rifles from me, and I will not take your country. This country is all bush, and no use to you. If you want wood and stone, you can get them here in plenty. There are also many ant-heaps. The sun is very hot. All you can get from me is war, nothing else. . . . We ask for God's blessing. God is with me as I write this. If you wish war, I am happy; if you wish peace, I am also content. But if you wish peace, go away from my country to your own.

Scarcely, one would think, the words of a madman. The Third Expedition had ended. But it was not to be peace, not for many years yet.

In the Nogal Valley, the Sayyid could afford to wait until the enemy attacked. In the meantime, he continued to extend his realm of influence among the tribes. Some he won by force, some by conversion, some by the power of his invective. He poured forth in his poems the promise of honour in this world or the next, the threat of the burning pit for the untrue. In *The Road to Damnation*, he compared the Somalis who were not with him to the members of the outcast Yibir people, sorcerers who practised the arts of divination, which, although frowned upon by the Muslim establishment, are still widely consulted.

> . . . it is their lot to trot in terror behind the infidel;
> They are fated to understand nothing and are condemned to madness.
> Their lot is to hate the faith and to despise the Divine Law;

Let them bring upon themselves a curse, those children of the devil.
It is their fate to bring sorrow to those who turn with
zeal to the holy war.
Outcast sorcerers are destined never to breathe the
sweet airs of heaven.

By the time the British organized the Fourth Expedition, they had finally come to realize that the success
of any desert operation depended upon transport. As
well as several thousand Somali camels, they now ac-
cumulated strong reinforcements at Berbera. The list
has a certain bizarre quality: 2,800 Indian camels
(which could carry heavier loads than the Somali
camels but needed watering more often); 700 Arabian
camels from Aden; 80 buck-wagons from South
Africa; 1,000 camels and 1,000 ponies from the Punjab
and the north west frontier of India. The sultry air of
Berbera must have been foully loud with the bawling
and moaning of these thousands of camels.

The Fourth Expedition moved out towards the
Nogal Valley in 1904. In an initial skirmish, between
relatively small reconnaissance parties on both sides,
the Sayyid's men won easily. Since the Sayyid was
believed to be concentrating most of his forces at
Jidbali, it was towards this spot that the British proceeded, with six Maxim guns and with troops who
were made up of English, Sikh, Punjabi, African,
Boer, and Somali.

When the two forces met, at Jidbali, the Sayyid was
estimated to have between six and eight thousand
skilled warriors, most of whom had rifles. The British
advanced in their usual square formation. The Dervishes' method was to move in short rushes, their
horses travelling at terrific speed, the clouds of red

Haud dust almost obscuring them as they closed in and fired. Then the warriors would whirl their horses around and withdraw, only to turn and charge again. But at Jidbali, it was the Maxim guns that ruled. Slashed by their fire, the Sayyid's warriors fell like scythed grass.

The Nogal Valley was now held by the British. Mahammed 'Abdille Hasan moved into Italian territory. This time his trek was known, and the path he took could be seen, for many of his men were wounded, his supplies were low, and his people were suffering from hunger and thirst. As they limped slowly northward they left a trail for the vultures. Dead men and women whom the others had not been strong enough to bury, dead children—very many of these—and camels and sheep that could not walk any further on the scorching sand.

Mahammed 'Abdille Hasan had a small garrison at Illig, in Italian Somaliland. It was to this place, therefore, that he now went, hoping to rebuild his forces. The British, however, gained Italian consent to land a force at Illig. They took the village without much difficulty, but the Dervishes were still holding out in two stone forts. Again, it was the Maxim guns that finally overcame the Sayyid's riflemen. The remnants of the Dervish fighters, together with their families, took shelter in the caves on the sea-facing cliffs and continued, amazingly, to fire upon the British from there. But ultimately they all lay dead, the last of the Illig garrison, and the British burned the village.

The fourth round had gone to the British. But the combined cost of the Third and Fourth Expeditions had been five million pounds. Moreover, although many of his warriors had been killed, Mahammed 'Abdille Hasan himself had not been captured and he had not surrendered.

The area around Illig was the Sayyid's base for the next three years. He signed a treaty with the Italians, in which he became an Italian-protected subject. In return he promised not to bring in any more rifles, although he could have had no intention of keeping the promise. The years that followed were a time for repairing strength, consolidation, and renewed attempts to win the full support of the Darod tribes of Somalis. He organized a network of spies who moved out into the Haud, searching for information and also seeking support, especially from the Dolbahanta and War-sangeli tribes. The Sayyid's instructions to his spies were often given in the form of *gabay*. The British countered with their own propaganda, for they needed to keep the Dolbahanta and Warsangeli as neutral tribes who would provide a kind of buffer between themselves and the Sayyid.

During this period, Mahammed 'Abdille Hasan exchanged many letters with Commissioner Cordeaux in Berbera. The Sayyid's letters are sharp-witted, sardonic, full of fire, wily and evasive at times, but holding always to his basic tenets of faith—*our land and our religion*. Often he would recast the essence of his letter to the British into the form of poetry, so the *gabay* could convey his views, his beliefs, his anger, to his own people. When Cordeaux complained that Mahammed 'Abdille Hasan was unfairly seeking to influence the Warsangeli, the Sayyid composed a *gabay* addressed to the English but intended for the ears of the Warsangeli:

Concerning your demand, "Turn aside from the War-
   sangeli," I have a complaint.
If they prefer you, then they and I shall be at variance.
It is not in my nature to accept people who cringe to
   you.
But if they are Dervishes, how can I turn aside from
   them?
Do you also share their ancestry from Darod?
Are you trying to steal towards me through my an-
   cestors?
Of late, have you not turned my people into gazelles,
   fugitive and homeless?
Have you not seen how they loathe you? . . .
You are building a mat partition between them and
   the streams of Paradise.
You are casting them into the raging fury and fumes
   of Hell.

The Warsangeli finally came in on his side. The
British had raised four expeditions, but they were not
rid of the Sayyid yet. The administration was growing more and more disturbed about this persistent
thorn in the imperial flesh. But the question was being
raised in the British Parliament—was holding on to
Somaliland really worth the expense involved? The
main posts in the interior—Hargeisa, Sheikh and Burao
—were being held by contingents of King's African
Rifles, but now the Sayyid's Dervish horsemen were
resuming their intermittent raids. The British made
arrangements to reinforce the k.a.r.'s with troops
from Aden, Nyasaland, and Uganda, but they seem
to have done so with considerable uneasiness. Would
the reinforcements prove sufficient even as a stop-gap
measure? Many British, both in Somaliland and at
home, believed not. Commissioner Cordeaux wrote to
the Sayyid, accusing him of raiding into British terri-

tory. After replying in Arabic to the British, Mahammed 'Abdille Hasan composed in his own language a reply which was to become a classic of Somali poetry, a poem filled with bitterness and yet possessing a sombre restraint.

> As to the raiders of whom you talk, I also have a complaint.
> It is you who have oppressed them and seized their beasts.
> It is you who took for yourselves their houses and property.
> It is you who spoilt their settlements and defiled them with ordure.
> It is you who reduced them to eating tortoise and beast of prey.
> This degradation you brought upon them.
> If they in turn become beasts of prey,
> Or steal small things from the clearings between your huts,
> Then they were driven to this by famine.
> Do not complain to me and I will not complain to you.

The British government finally decided against a full-scale expedition as being too expensive. Completely leaving Somaliland, however, would have meant a severe loss of prestige, they felt, and would also have left the coastal ports open to some other European power. At last, in 1909, the British decided upon a compromise solution. They withdrew all their forces from the interior of Somaliland and occupied only the coastal ports of Berbera and Zeilah.

In 1910, in the British House of Commons, the government soothingly stated that the power of the Mad Mullah was now completely broken. But in 1911, Mahammed 'Abdille Hasan attacked the Dolbahanta, took their stock, and moved again into the pasture lands of the Nogal Valley. Tales reached the British in Berbera that the Sayyid was becoming more ruthless with the dissenting tribes, that he was mutilating prisoners, and that the few remaining neutral tribes of the interior, whether out of belief in his goals or fear of his strength, were fast coming under his control. The holy war had been resumed.

The British countered by forming the Somali Camel Constabulary to maintain order within fifty miles of the coast. This group later became the famous Somaliland Camel Corps, a military detachment, but in its early days it was a civilian body. It was commanded by Richard Corfield, who was to become a legendary figure in the history of Somaliland. Corfield had been a political officer in Somaliland for some years, and then had been transferred to Nigeria. He belonged to that small but distinctive sect of Englishmen who could be really happy only in the desert, living among desert people. He found in the Somalis a toughness and an ability to survive, combined with a reckless courage—qualities which produced a deep response in his own nature. When he was offered the chance to return to Somaliland and command the new Camel Constabulary, he accepted enthusiastically. He could hardly wait to take his new force out, but for a full year the 150 men, all crack shots, were trained and organized, for despite his impatience Corfield was determined that this force would be a spectacular one.

In the Haud, news of Corfield and his Camel Constabulary reached Mahammed 'Abdille Hasan. He feared another expedition, for his own army was not yet strong enough. He wrote to the British, suggesting talks and signing himself, "From the slave of God, and the poor man, bin 'Abdille Hasan." The British agreed to meet him, but this encounter never took place, for both sides quibbled too much over the place and terms of meeting.

Things were not going well for the Sayyid. He had won over to his side many of the interior tribes, but their men were untrained and he did not know how far he could trust them in battle. His own picked troops, the young warriors, the true Dervishes who were prepared to die in his cause, were not sufficient in numbers. He needed a base much more impregnable than the Nogal Valley, where he could train new warriors and withstand a heavy attack. He decided to move once more.

He settled on Taleh in the eastern Haud as his head-quarters and began building a fortress there. He brought in Arab stonemasons from the Yemen, for the Somalis had never built in stone. He himself had no experience of building on such a scale, but he designed and planned and saw take shape a large walled main enclosure, surrounded by thirteen forts, with three covering forts. The walls were all from twelve to fourteen feet thick at the base, and the covering forts were some sixty feet high.

Early in 1913, Richard Corfield took his Camel Constabulary out to Burao and managed to settle a good deal of intertribal fighting. They stayed until summer, when Corfield at last obtained the government's agreement to take his force out to Ber, where the Dervishes had been raiding. Corfield's instructions were explicit, and they were not much to his liking. He was not to engage in attack with any large number of Dervishes. If Mahammed 'Abdille Hasan's men were encountered in any strength, Corfield was to return immediately to Burao. Captain Summers, of the 26th King George's Own Light Cavalry, was to accompany Corfield as military adviser. Corfield's only consolation was that Summers was not to interfere.

On August 8, the Camel Constabulary, just over a hundred men on fast riding camels, left Burao. On the road to Ber they met fleeing Dolbahanta tribesmen who reported that a large Dervish raiding party was attacking all the encampments in the area. The Camel Constabulary camped for the night, and when the darkness came, they were able to see the lights of the Dervish campfires all around them.

Corfield seems to have spent the night arguing with himself—or, rather, discovering logical reasons for what he had already decided to do. He was determined to attack, despite his orders. As soon as it was dawn, they moved out. The land was covered with dense thorny bushes in that immediate area, and the men on their riding camels saw nothing of the Dervishes, not a sign, although far away, on the line of the low hills, they could see the hovering dust clouds that were being raised by the captured Dolbahanta camels. They arrived at Dul Madoba, the Black Hill. Corfield ordered his men to dismount and form a line. He intended to move them gradually beyond the thicket and onto the nearby plain.

Then, startlingly, the sound of hooves. The Dervish horsemen were crossing the plain at colossal speed. Captain Summers advised Corfield to form the constabulary rapidly into a square, but Corfield refused because this formation would have lessened the extent of his fire.

The Dervishes thundered in, chanting their battle cry—*Mahammed Saalih!* The constabulary's one Maxim gun was knocked out by rifle fire, and the hundred men were soon entirely surrounded by Dervish horsemen. Retreat was not possible now.

Corfield, the young Englishman who had desired so desperately, so strangely, to lead his small band into battle, however outnumbered they might be, was given his chance—his first and his last. He met the onthrusting Dervishes, and he led his men, just as he had always wanted to do. Then he was shot through the head, and died instantly.

Captain Summers took over. A grotesque wall had been formed with the bodies of dead camels and horses, and for five hours the constabulary kept firing from behind this shelter. If the Dervishes had closed in, and had stayed, the constabulary would have been completely destroyed. But the Sayyid's men kept to their traditional battle action—short swift rushes, followed by withdrawal, and then another assault. Finally and inexplicably, they withdrew entirely. Of the Camel Constabulary, only twenty-three men remained.

Among Somalis, the battle of Dul Madoba became known as "The Day of the Grinding of Bones." Mahammed 'Abdille Hasan composed a *gabay* on this victory. The poem has an exultant rage in it. Corfield's death throes are exaggerated, as though the Sayyid were compelled to draw out his enemy's suffering, to linger over it in hate-filled detail.

You have died, Corfield, and are no longer in this world.
A merciless journey was your portion.
When, Hell-destined, you set out for the Other World

Those who have gone to Heaven will question you,
if God is willing,
When you see the companions of the faithful and the
jewels of Heaven,
Answer them how God tried you.
Say to them: "With fervour and faith the Dervishes
attacked us."
Report how savagely their swords tore you.
Say: "As I looked fearfully from side to side, my
heart was plucked from its sheath."
Say: "My eyes stiffened as I watched with horror;
The mercy I implored was not granted."
Say: "Striking with spear-butts at my mouth they
silenced my soft words."
Say: "The schemes the djinns planted in me brought
my ruin."
Say: "Great shouts acclaimed the departing of my
soul."
Say: "Beasts of prey have eaten my flesh and torn it
apart for meat."
Say: "The Dervishes are like the advancing thunder-
bolts of a storm."

After Dul Madoba, the British decided to re-occupy
the interior of Somaliland. The Dervish raids continued, however, and the Sayyid even struck at Berbera itself, the furthest point from his own sphere of
influence, the very heart of the British administration.
Undetected by government troops at any of the outposts, forty of the Sayyid's best horsemen, mounted on
the swiftest of the Dervish ponies, rode across the
wide Haud, through the Sheikh Hills, across the tree-
less coastal plain of the Guban, and into carefully
guarded Berbera. It was a symbolic act. The Dervishes
fired a few shots around the *magala*, the Somali part of
the town, caused near-hysteria among the local in-

habitants, and galloped off again. But they had scored their point. Berbera felt secure no longer.

The Camel Constabulary was re-organized on military lines and named the Somaliland Camel Corps. Their first action was to attack three Dervish forts at Shimber Berris in the hills and to dynamite them.

After the fall of the Shimber Berris forts, Mahammed 'Abdille Hasan concentrated his whole strength at Taleh, his headquarters. Rumours of his plans and his potential reached the British through the coast tribes in their seasonal migrations to and from the Haud, where they took their camels for grazing. The rumours, as always, were wildly contradictory. The Sayyid's armies were growing mightily, and a serious attack on Berbera was planned. The Sayyid's armies had dwindled, and he was finding it difficult to obtain arms and ammunition.

What the real picture was, it is impossible to say, but it seems certain that Mahammed 'Abdille Hasan had relinquished none of his aims of a unified Somaliland under Muslim rule. He was still recruiting among the tribes, and the war *gabay* still poured forth—poetry portraying battle in heroic terms, in much the same way as Homer made splendid in words the tribal battles of the ancient Greeks, and, like Homer, picturing the courageous warrior as noblest among men.

When the cries for help rise up
And when arms are taken to the fields of battle
And when the bay horse wades through the sand and
    dust,
On that day when men break their spears in chest and
    spine,
When the vulture falls upon the spewed-out meat,

And when the din of battle resounds all around,
When the coward drops his weapons and abandons
    you for flight—
On that day is not he who fights bravely like a lion
    attacking?

But another and infinitely more vast war was to
draw the attention of the British completely away
from Somaliland. When the First World War began,
the outposts of empire had to be largely forgotten.
From 1914 to 1918 the Somaliland situation was
shelved by Britain. Somaliland was still occupied, but
the British made no attacks on Mahammed 'Abdille
Hasan. The Sayyid, for his part, continued his spo-
radic raids, but oddly enough made no major move.
Perhaps his strength had been dissipated in the innumerable small attacks on the uncommitted tribes.
Perhaps he no longer believed, in his heart, after nearly
two decades of fighting, that the *Jihad*, his holy war,
could succeed. Perhaps he did not realize the extent
to which the British were involved elsewhere. In any
event, he played a waiting game.

At the conclusion of the Great War, the British
once more focused attention on their empire. In 1920,
a full-scale military and aerial expedition was launched
in Somaliland. It was to be the last. The forces which
were to move against the desert leader included: the
fourteen planes of Z Unit, R.A.F.; the Somaliland Camel
Corps (700 rifles); a battalion of King's African Rifles
(700 rifles); half a battalion of Grenadiers, Indian
Army (400 rifles); an irregular Somali levy (1500
rifles); Illaloes or Somali tribal police (300 rifles).

In January the planes delivered the first air attack
on the Sayyid's forts at Taleh. The reports that fil-

tered through to the British afterwards paint a disturbing picture. Mahammed 'Abdille Hasan was a warrior by tradition, an able strategist in desert warfare. But he did not know of the existence of aviation. When the planes came over his forts, he did not know what to expect. He assumed that they bore, in some fashion mysterious to him, emissaries from his enemies who wished to talk with him. He therefore put on his finest clothes, his white robes and embroidered silk turban. He walked out and sat under the white canopy used on important occasions. He was older now, and not only in years. Possibly it showed in his face—the battles that never ended, the deaths of so many of his sons. But he would have looked as haughty as ever, still the same zeal burning in him. He awaited the messengers. Then the first bomb fell.

The air attacks went on for three days, with bombing and machine-gunning. The forts were set on fire by incendiary bombs. Meantime, the British ground forces were attacking an outlying fort at Baran, some miles away. The Dervishes there held out all through the night, shouting curses at the British. The Sayyid's men had spears and rifles; the British had Stokes guns. In the morning, the British succeeded in blowing up the fort. Some of the Dervishes kept on firing until shot at close range with revolvers. None surrendered.

The Camel Corps took Jidali, another outlying fort, using Stokes guns, hand grenades, and explosives. Methods of war had changed since Corfield's day. The Dervishes held out, firing and singing—singing "*Miraculous man of God, Mahammed Saalih*"—until they were all dead. No prisoners were taken. There were none to take.

Mahammed 'Abdille Hasan himself was not captured when Taleh was bombed. He is said to have shared his pony with his favourite wife as he slipped through the British lines and got away to the south. The Camel Corps and the King's African Rifles followed the Sayyid's retreat, while the R.A.F. bombed the bands of Dervishes who were trying to escape with their families and their livestock. Warriors, women, children, camels and sheep—death came from the air for all of them.

Eventually, the Camel Corps captured the Sayyid's wives and children and most of the remaining Dervish horsemen. But the Sayyid himself crossed the Haud somehow and got into Ethiopian territory.

The campaign had lasted only three weeks. The British sent Mahammed 'Abdille Hasan a letter, offering him immunity from punishment if he would surrender. The Sayyid replied in a magnificent and heartbroken document which must have cost him a very great deal to write.

These words are from the man who is oppressed, bin 'Abdille Hasan, to the oppressors without cause. . . . You say that the Dervishes have become weak and I am alone without following, all my people having run away; that on your side you have lost but one man, while many of mine have been killed; and that you have caught all my intimates, relatives and family; and that you have beaten the Turks and the Germans. And then you tell me to rejoin my people, otherwise you will not let me be. That is the meaning of what you have written. . . .

And to this I reply. To what you have said about the Dervishes growing weak I can say nothing, neither yes nor no. Allah is Almighty, and if He desires to confer power or to weaken, it is for Him to do so.

You say my people have run away. My answer is yes. Some of my people have run away and some will never leave me until I die. But those who have left me will be no use to you. . . .

And now, if you want to offer me terms, then let me be myself among the people. But if you are not agreeable to this—then I want the right to place my case before you and I want justice from the people. And if there is anything proved against me, then I have no complaint to make. And by this means, if I have my rights, I shall be satisfied, and I shall never get up again. . . .

This, and salaams.

The British, astonishingly, interpreted this letter as being noncommittal and written only to gain time. They persisted in their dual and contradictory view of the man they called the Mad Mullah. On the one hand, they visualized him as utterly insane, while on the other hand they believed him to be not only wrong in his uprisings but also fully aware of his wrongness. At that point in history, their deeply ingrained imperialism did not permit them to see him as a nationalist leader with a legitimate aim, a man whose alleged slaughter of innocents certainly could not have equalled their own, not after the Taleh bombing and strafing.

This letter of the Sayyid's now seems a peculiarly revealing one. He was beaten and he acknowledged it. He acknowledged that many of his people had deserted him. He acknowledged even the last bitterness —that God, after all, might not have intended to confer power upon him, that the war for his land and his religion might not, in the book of Heaven, ever have been marked for success. It had been twenty years. After Taleh, he must have felt himself to be a man utterly bereft. He asks only that the Somali people judge him. And if they reject him, in the final analysis, then "I shall never get up again." Far from being the letter of a madman, or of a man stalling for time, this document seems the work of a man who was capable of facing the truly tragic circumstances of his life.

Did his mind break, though, at the very end? It seems to have done. Almost the last word we have of him is the report of the delegation of Somali sheikhs who were sent by the British on an impossible mission to try to make some final treaty. When it was first suggested to these sheikhs, all of whom were dignitaries and men of responsibility in their own communities, that they should travel into Ethiopia and interview the Sayyid, one of their number hastily excused himself from the gathering in Government House and rushed out to the veranda, where he vomited in pure panic. The Sayyid might be defeated and broken, but his name was still powerful.

Numerous blood-chilling reports preceded the return of the sheikhs from the Sayyid's encampment, and all this highly dramatic situation makes us query the final report they gave. Almost certainly, they were not going to spoil a good story by adhering too closely to the realities. At the same time, some of the details of their encounter with Mahammed 'Abdille Hasan seem to bear a convincing ring of truth.

The Sayyid, it must be remembered, had never been seen by the British. When the sheikhs returned, their description of his physical appearance was the description of a mythical figure, not an actual man. He was much more than six feet tall, they claimed, and enormously fat, but nonetheless a man of supreme strength. He was richly robed in white silk, and his skin was

assan, the copper colour most favoured by Somalis.
But while this description seems to owe more to the
eyes of the beholders than it does to the subject, the
sheikhs observed other things which seem more likely.
The Sayyid was attended by only a hundred riflemen,
and these were mostly old men, clad in ragged robes.
The retinue of a fallen king. Mahammed 'Abdille
Hasan abused and tormented the sheikhs, they reported irritably (and this sounds like him), by making
them wait interminably and by not addressing them
by their proper names.

He insisted upon displaying, according to the
sheikhs—and this is so moving and so terrible that it
may well be true—his skill as a horseman, for their
eyes. He mounted an old swayback, and jerked the
curb so that the horse reared very slightly.

"I always have to break in all our young Dervish
horses," the Sayyid said.

The final sight of him is the letter he wrote, during
his exile, to Governor Archer. Now he was truly
broken. The man who had fought for twenty years
could fight no longer. The man who could perceive
and acknowledge tragedy had died. The body that
still lived had no aims now in the real world—it had
been forced at last into the refuge of dreams. He
wrote to Archer to demand the return of his treasure,
none of which existed except in his imagination. Both
the list and the accompanying letter make painful
reading.

> Golden coins amounting to £100,000.
> The feathers are the feathers of 900 ostriches.
> Other small coins not counted.
> Twenty boxes of scent.
> Five boxes of diamonds.

A thousand pearls.
Two pieces of ivory.
Very many firearms. . . .

And the letter:

Oh Governor Archer! I am Sayyid Mahammed! I
know you! You attacked me and I am oppressed. The
airplanes have oppressively attacked me, and this is a
great abuse to a man in my position. You have also
killed forty of my children. . . .

One cannot bear to read on, to see any more of the
breaking of a man. He had held out far beyond the
powers of most men, and in an age in which his
concepts were unacceptable and misunderstood, even
to a large extent among his own people. He ought to
have died in battle, but this death was not granted to
him. His encampment in Ethiopia shrunk; those who
were loyal to the end grew poorer. Mercifully, however, the end was not long in coming. He died in
December 1920, and it was said he died either of malaria or influenza, but probably, whatever the immediate cause, he died because there was no longer any
reason for him to go on living.

How far did the British attitude to Mahammed
'Abdille Hasan correspond to reality? Only at a much
later date could any colonial power find itself opposed
and withdraw after due process of preparation. At the
time of the Sayyid, the assumption was that anyone
who opposed the administration was quite obviously
an enemy of the people. That the Somali people themselves were in large numbers against the British rule
was something the British never for one instant believed. Mahammed 'Abdille Hasan was coercing the

tribes into supporting him, the British thought and continued to think for twenty years. It is difficult to see how thousands upon thousands of nomadic tribesmen, spread over an area of some hundreds of miles, could have been sufficiently intimidated over a long period in any way that would make them useful to the Sayyid. They could be attacked, of course, and in some cases were, but the Sayyid was after support, not dead men. The fact that in the major campaigns he was supported by so many followers drawn from a wide range of tribes, and that his armies included not only men from the Darod tribes but often from the Isaaq as well, seems now to indicate that his uprising represented a grass-roots rebellion of considerable proportions.

The British views on the character of the Sayyid were even more strongly tinged with fantasy. These views can be most clearly observed in *The Mad Mullah of Somaliland* by Douglas Jardine, who was chief secretary to the Protectorate government through part of the Dervish wars and whose book gives almost the only detailed account of the campaigns. Jardine's description of the battles is factual and drawn from reports of the time, but his picture of the "Mullah" is flamboyant in the extreme. The British appear to have seen the Sayyid as a kind of grossly exaggerated Arabian Nights figure—unvaryingly and diabolically cruel, a profligate of the worst order, a man who spent his days and nights in riotous living, a glutton and a lecher in the grand style.

If we consider Mahammed 'Abdille Hasan within his cultural framework, a warrior reared in a rigid tribal system which equated mercy towards anyone other than kinsmen as weakness, it seems highly likely that he did have spies summarily put to death and that he tortured them not only to gain information but also as an outlet for the consuming rage he felt towards his enemies. He himself, in his poetry, occasionally reveals a cruelty which verges on hysteria—"I meant to cut off the testicles of the menstruating infidels"— the paradoxical desire to unsex these men who simultaneously were not acknowledged as men. But as far as his profligacy is concerned, it does not seem probable that the Sayyid, who preached the strict Saalihiya doctrines until the day he died, should have so far departed from them in his own life. It is also difficult to see how, if he was as debauched as the British claimed, he managed to fight on for so long and to rally his forces again and again.

As for the Sayyid's supposed insanity, it seems obvious now that the British believed him mad because they had to believe him mad and had to believe themselves and their own policies impeccably sane. In Jardine's book, Mahammed 'Abdille Hasan is sometimes termed "His Madness"— he who must be given a title, and so the title given is one of supreme contempt. To the British administrators of that day, the very fact that an African leader would oppose the Raj was almost in itself sufficient evidence of his insanity. Also, the reports of the Sayyid which reached the administration were all from Somalis who sided with the British, and it is reasonable to assume that they would say things which they felt the administration would want to hear. The picture which the British received was undoubtedly that of a man whose mind was so unhinged that he was in a constant state of raving. The British accepted this image because it was the one they desperately needed, not only to justify their policies but perhaps also in some way to tame their own fears of him.

The facts are few enough, but they are fairly telling. Mahammed 'Abdille Hasan's letters to the British are written in an intense but exceedingly lucid prose, and the two main branches of his belief are expressed with complete consistency—his land should be free of a foreign administration, and should be ruled by Muslims. His poetry contains fury and violence, but it could never be called the work of a depraved mind. Only at the end, when everything he had staked his life upon had been shattered, does his mind seem to have ceased to grapple.

The mingling of reality and fantasy also characterized the Somalis' view of the Sayyid, both those who supported him and those who held back. They were tribal men, brought up in the belief that the sultan was he who was absolutely strong, even mystically strong. The power of the Somali chiefs had been taken over by the British—infidels though they were, they were the Authority now. To revolt against an authority which you unconsciously believe to be in some way unassailable demands not only an act of will but also an act of the greatest faith, and it is never done without paying a terrible price in anxiety and pain. I believe that Mahammed 'Abdille Hasan himself had reached this point of no return, the point at which he was compelled, because he was Somali and Muslim, to rise up against an authority which was alien and infidel. But I do not think he could possibly have done so without a great deal of uncertainty, a concealed and irrational uncertainty, but an anguish nonetheless, and I believe that his followers must have gone through the same unacknowledged torment. Even those Somalis who cast their lot with the British must have experienced a damaging dichotomy of mind—they had gambled on the authority they felt to be the most secure, but they were never certain. Many of those who did not actually support the Sayyid seem to have believed at least half the time that he would triumph, and even those who were always opposed to him on grounds of tribal differences appear to have believed that he possessed supernatural powers.

These tales of more-than-earthly strength are an interesting sidelight on the Sayyid's career. Immediately after the first symbolic raid on Burao, the rumours began. In the manner of desert dwellers, these rumours were passed from campfire to campfire, from well to well, and it was impossible to know who had started them. But this kind of whisper is begun only by those who need to believe, who must believe for their own inner safety. Mahammed 'Abdille Hasan, it was said, possessed an amulet with lifesaving powers, a charm which had been bestowed upon him by a *shaitan*, a devil, whose familiar was a she-lizard whose life had once been saved by the Sayyid.

The British quieted their own fantasy fears of the sensual giant who threatened their neatly buttoned control and decent officialdom, by declaring the fellow mad. The followers of Mahammed 'Abdille Hasan, similarly, quieted their submerged fears of an unshakeable Authority by declaring that their leader possessed supernatural powers of protection. They believed he had the power to turn the bullets of the infidel into water, a belief which persisted even when proved fallible. This belief, in exactly the same form, has been observed in the early and generally unsuccessful rebellions of peoples in colonial situations in other parts of the world. O. Mannoni, the French psychologist, in *The Psychology of Colonization*, describes precisely the same thing in the uprising of the Malagasy people in Madagascar in 1947, when the cry of the stick-armed Malagasies was *"Rano, Rano"*—Rain—the conviction that the bullets of the rifles that stood against them would turn to water. Mannoni believes that as a magical device this bullets-into-water concept indicates at an unconscious level the necessity of a tribal man, reared within the secure firmness of his own cultural authority and compelled to act violently against the now-prevailing colonialist authority, to visualize his opponent as impotent. The rifle, symbol of the male sex organ, is reduced to the capability of the man-child, where the penis produces nothing more potent than water.

The recourse to magic in one form or another is common in battles in which an essentially tribal people are faced with an enemy which has not a superior culture but only more efficient weapons, more efficient means of killing. At Culloden, in 1746, when the Highland clans were being slaughtered by the British cannon, many of them threw down their rifles, unfired, and attacked with the weapon of their ancestors, the claymore. And in 1885, when the prairie Métis faced the armies from Upper Canada and General Middleton's cannon, they believed that their leader, Louis Riel, had the ability to see through walls and the gift of turning away bullets by the power of the large cross which he held aloft.

The parallels between Riel and the Sayyid extend much further than this desperate recourse to magic.

The question of Riel's sanity or insanity has long been argued, and although the circumstances of the two men's lives and struggles are very different, it seems to me that there are many common threads: both were the leaders of communities of basically tribal and nomadic people (the camel herders of Somaliland; the Métis buffalo hunters of the Canadian prairies) faced with imperialist and colonialist powers which possessed only one superior quality, namely superior means of slaughter, and which intended to take over the people's land and the administration thereof. The mental stress and grief of such a leader must have been terrible. One main difference in the two men's alleged insanity is, of course, that Riel ultimately played the grotesque pageant through to its end with sanity and in plain view of the world—his death on the scaffold in Regina. His most intense moments of alienation from reality occurred at the final defeat of his people at Batoche in 1885, when he was clearly looking for miraculous solutions. But his last will and testament, his last letters, and his final words are plainly the work of a perfectly lucid mind. The Sayyid, on the other hand, escaped a dramatic death and lived on, tragically, to see his forces and his own powers dwindling into pathos.

The superstitions attached to Mahammed 'Abdille Hasan by the Somalis reveal the degree of anxiety that must have been experienced by the Dervish forces and by the Sayyid himself. In a reverse way, also, they show the compulsive strength of a movement which could rise, take shape, be defeated, rally, reform and go on fighting for twenty years despite not only the outer circumstances but the inner storms as well.

74

Mahammed 'Abdille Hasan was not a simple man. He was not a man who could be summed up in a few words. He used his own words as implements of war, and in themselves they were a form of assault. Yet one of his best-known *gabay* expresses the deeply affectionate concern over the departure of a friend on a hazardous journey.

Now you depart, and though your way may lead
Through airless forests, thick with *hhagar* trees,
Places steeped in heat, stifling and dry,
Where breath comes hard, and no fresh breeze can
    reach—
Yet may God place a shield of coolest air
Between your body and the assailant sun.

And in a random scorching flame of wind
That parches the painful throat and sears the flesh,
May God, in His compassion, let you find
The great-boughed tree that will protect and shade.

On every side of you, I now would place
Prayers from the Holy Qoran, to bless your path,
That ills may not descend, nor evils harm,
And you may travel in the peace of faith.
To all the blessings I bestow on you,
Friend, yourself now say a last Amen.

He was a man of his time, but some of his concepts went beyond his time. A contemporary Somali poet has described him as "the man who fought against great odds." That he did, and in the end he failed but did not fail. His battles demonstrated so decisively his people's adherence to their religion that Christian missions did not operate there henceforth. His determination inspired advocates of Somali independence from that time forward. His country is now the

Somali Republic, an independent Muslim state.

It might seem a heresy, from his point of view, to describe Mahammed 'Abdille Hasan in the words of any Christian. But the world has changed, and perhaps now the words of one faith may occasionally be related to another faith. The Sayyid might have recognized, through all the stone walls of separate dogma, the words of St. Paul, excessively proud and yet in some final way humble—"I have fought a good fight; I have finished my course; I have kept the faith."

Enigmatic as this Somali warrior and poet remains —for in the end we cannot separate the man from the myth—this at least can be said of him. He fought a good fight; he finished his course; he kept the faith.

SOURCES

B.W. Andrzejewski and I.M. Lewis. *Somali Poetry: An Introduction.* London: Oxford University Press, 1964.

Douglas Jardine. *The Mad Mullah of Somaliland.* London: Herbert Jenkins, 1923.

Margaret Laurence. *A Tree for Poverty.* Nairobi: Eagle Press, 1954; reprinted by Irish University Press and McMaster University Press, 1970.

O. Mannoni. *The Psychology of Colonization.* London: Methuen, 1956.

This article is a re-telling of the many tales about this Somali poet I heard when I was working on translations of Somali poems and folk-tales, with the help of my friends Musa Haji Ismail Galaal and B. W. Andrzejewski. This tale may be myth, in the sense that it has undoubtedly become changed over the years and been given a kind of dramatic splendour missing from the original events, but myths contain their own truth, their own strong reality.

The Epic Love of Elmii Bonderii

"He died of love," the Somalis say. "Absolutely nothing else."

The minarets of the mosque stand thin and wax-white as candles in the burning air, and around them the town of Berbera swelters beside the murky, greenish blue of the Gulf of Aden. Inland, the scorched plains of the Guban lead to the dark jaggedness of the Sheikh Hills, and beyond the hills stretches the harsh plateau of the Haud, the earth hard and unyielding as red granite, the high rust-coloured termite mounds like grotesque sculptures, the few twisted trees bearing always their spears of thorn. Camel-herding nomads sometimes walk a hundred miles between one well and the next, and in the almost unendurable drought of the *Jilal* season, tribal wars still flare, as they have for countless centuries, over water. A man might easily die of thirst here, or he might die in battle. But to die of love? Here, where life is so elemental?

Yet the story is true, as any Somali will tell you,

77

and indeed Elmii Bonderii's way of death is not the aspect of the tale that surprises them most. The real strangeness is how such a man as Elmii Bonderii ever became a poet—not just any poet, either, but one of the most skilled, in a land that values its bards and judges them by strict literary standards.

A long tradition of poetry exists among Somalis, but because their language has not, until recently, been a written one, poems are transmitted orally and their life is limited. Most poems fall like leaves, seasonally, and a new crop takes their place. Only the work of the best poets survives and is passed on, from generation to generation, with remarkable accuracy. The poems of Elmii Bonderii seem likely to last, for it is nearly thirty years since the young poet's death and his work is still very much alive in the Somali Republic. When a poem is recited, the circumstances of the composition are always recounted, so the history of Elmii Bonderii goes on, as well, and people still ponder over the mystery that brought out such richness in the life of so unlikely a man.

He was not anyone you would have noticed if you had seen him in the days before his fate seized him. He was in his early thirties, an undistinguished man who did not have cleverness or good looks or wealth. He was unexceptional in every way. His name meant Elmii the Borderman, for he had been born near the Ethiopian border. As a young man, however, he had left the camel-herding life of the desert and gone to work in a teashop in Berbera.

Somali teashops are centres of social life. They are nothing much to look at—huts of mud brick, or clay and wattle, roofed with corrugated tin. Inside are low wooden benches and tables where mugs of sweet spiced tea are served. In the late afternoons and evenings, the teashops buzz with news and politics, argument and discussion, scandal and poetry. Here the young men sing the love songs they have composed, and if a song catches the listening ears, soon everyone will be singing it.

> He who has lain between her breasts
> Can call his life fulfilled.
> Oh God, may I never be denied
> The well of happiness.

But when the serious poems begin, the young men are silenced. Simple love songs are fine for those who are young in years or mentality, but the poems of the elders are the *gabay*, long and intricate, following complex rules of composition, full of theological and genealogical allusions. These are the vehicles of political persuasion, personal invective, admonition, philosophical speculation. Through the *gabay*, a man can express what is closest to his heart and mind—his grief, his rage, his faith, his love, his resolution.

Elmii Bonderii took no part in the activities of the teashop. He did his work, but that was all. He never composed his own songs, as so many of the young men did, and when the audience began making critical comments on the latest offering of a *gabay*-maker, he had nothing to say. No one remembers his having shown much interest in poetry or even in talk of any description, and this in itself is unusual among Somalis, who are nothing if not vociferous.

All the same, he must have listened. Perhaps he

heard some of the famous *gabay*-makers of that time chanting their own poems—Abdillaahi Muuse, with his scathing *Elder's Reproof to His Wife* ("a fool's mind is like a house barred") or even the great Salaan Arrabey, whose long anguished outcry against a faithless friend is one of the classics of Somali literature.

> Fortune is my scourge;
> Would ye have me keep my peace and make no cry?
> This is the way of life, this bitter way—
> Kindness towards men begets their secret hate.

Elmii must have heard, too, some impassioned reciter chanting the poems of the greatest *gabay*-maker of all, Sayyid Mahammed 'Abdille Hasan, the early nationalist leader who was known to the British as the Mad Mullah of Somaliland. War is one of the main themes of Somali *gabay*, and the war poetry of the Sayyid is strong, bloody, and uncompromising.

> And when the bay horse wades through the sand and
>   dust,
> On that day when men break their spears in chest and
>   spine,
> When the vulture falls upon the spewed-out meat . . .

The sheer force and sweep of it is sometimes reminiscent of Homer, whose subject was also tribal war and who described it in similar terms of elevated drama, grandeur, and gore. Even someone who took hardly any notice of the poems that went spinning like verbal spears around the teashop in the evenings couldn't have ignored the war *gabay* of the Sayyid. If such poems had any effect on Elmii Bonderii, however, he never revealed it. No one would have said he had the possibility of poetry in him.

But no man can avoid his fate, the Somalis believe. One day, in the streets of Berbera, Elmii caught sight of a girl named Hodan. She was by no means the most beautiful girl in the land, nor even in Berbera. In fact, she was rather plain. But as soon as Elmii Bonderii saw her, he loved her, absolutely and totally. He went to the girl's family and begged to be allowed to marry her. But as he had virtually no money, they refused.

"What if I earn enough to pay the *yarad*, the bride-wealth?" he asked. "Would you let me marry Hodan then?"

They would consider it, the family replied. The girl was only fifteen years old, and they were in no hurry for her to marry. Elmii gave up his job at the teashop and departed for Djibouti, in French Somaliland, where wages were higher. For several years he worked on the docks as a labourer, and at last he saved enough for the bride-wealth. With his cash and his hopes, he returned to Berbera.

But he had stayed away too long. Hodan was already married, to a man whose ominous name was Mohamed Shabel—Mohamed the Leopard. For weeks Elmii walked around in a state of intense depression. Finally, unable to free himself of his obsessive passion for Hodan, he fell ill.

It was then that the inexplicable transformation took place. As though a piece of Haud rock had turned overnight into silver, in his illness Elmii Bonderii suddenly became a poet.

Among Somalis, no one becomes a poet suddenly. Young poets go through a period of apprenticeship, composing short lyric songs, before tackling the long and difficult *gabay*. The status of a good *gabay* poet is extremely high, but he is expected to produce something worth listening to, and his audience will deride him if they think his poetry is slapdash or not cleverly expressed. Many words used in *gabay* are not part of ordinary Somali speech, and a young poet has to master the use of this literary language before he tries to launch himself as a *gabay*-maker. There is no formal instruction, and the process of learning by doing usually takes years, even when a poet has considerable natural talent. Elmii Bonderii bypassed this arduous practice period. He began with the most complicated poetic form of all, and although the poems were chanted quite spontaneously—and indeed seemed to pour out of him—they fulfilled all the requirements of the *gabay* tradition: the tricky alliteration, the knowledge of Islamic law, the sonorous dignity, and sombre tone that typify the *gabay*.

All his poems were about Hodan. One of these was called *Qaraami*, which means "passionate." In it he describes her with great tenderness, speaking of her fine-shaped bones, her graceful bearing, her features:

> A careless flickering of her eyes
> Begets a light clear as the white spring moon.
> My heart leaps when I see her walking by.

He did not, of course, actually see her walking by. He could not see her at all, for now she led the protected and almost shut-away life of a married woman.

The poem has the quality of dream and fantasy. He imagines that he is married to her, and that he has even divorced another wife in order to marry Hodan. He speaks touchingly of her household skills—"Her strong hands weave the mats and tend the fire"—as though seeking to assure himself that she has attributes more lasting than physical beauty. With gentle irony the poem ends in an expression of sympathy for his audience:

> When you behold my incomparable one,
> Your own wives, in your eyes, will all be old.
> Alas, alas, for ye who hear my song!

The friends who came to visit Elmii were impressed by this spate of poetry. As he recited, they memorized his *gabay* and then repeated them in the teashops of the town. Soon the poems of Elmii Bonderii and the story of his love had spread to villages and encampments of nomads far across the desert.

Within a few months, he had achieved an enormous popularity. Many people who were unknown to him came to visit and to pray for his recovery. But Elmii showed no signs of recovering. The local doctor claimed there was nothing wrong with him, but Elmii thought otherwise. Perhaps he had made up his mind to die, and was not to be deterred by pills or pleas or prayers. His weird intensity seemed like some kind of inertia, a force that, having begun, could not stop but had to keep on, compulsively. Or had his sudden acclaim as the poet of epic love thrust him into a bizarre role from which there was no turning back?

"Only Allah knows," the Somalis say, "and only Allah can judge."

His friends, understandably, became a little impatient with him. The whole thing had been fine for a while, very startling, and with some good *gabay* to show for it, God knows how. But wasn't it time for the game to stop? Plenty of men fell in love and failed to get the girl. It wasn't the end of the world. Couldn't Elmii be quiet about it for a change? He replied with a poem, addressed to Hodan, which said in part:

> Oh daughter of a Sultan, when camels graze at night,
> And when the males cannot find the she-camels,
> They do not keep silent, but call through the darkness.

The crowds multiplied as Elmii grew sicker. Some came in the hope of hearing one of the now-famous poems flowering mysteriously from the mouth of a man who still seemed nondescript. Some came to console him with the wisdom of the Qoran. And some, naturally, came to inform him that he was faking his malady in order to get himself noticed, or that he was mad, or that he was possessed not by love but by a *shaitan*—a devil. To these, Elmii responded with some bitterness, but in a poem which is nonetheless a praise of love.

> Long ago, God the Just created women for love.
> Love came to the lordly man, who shone with the
>   radiance of God's throne . . .
> Mankind was divided into male and female
> So that they might be inspired with wonder at each
>   other.

If it had not been so, they would not have spread
  from a desolate place,
And the Somalis in their evil custom would not have
  mocked me.

Elmii's friends now moved from half-sceptical irri-
tation to genuine dismay. They were, after all, fond
of him, incomprehensible though he might be. The
fool might actually die unless something were done,
and done quickly. They sent out an appeal, asking the
loveliest girls in the country to come and present
themselves out of concern for the poet. Surely some
girl, somewhere, would please Elmii and ultimately
take Hodan's place in his heart.

The response was staggering. From Berbera and
Hargeisa they came, from the dry plains of the Haud
and from the distant fishing villages around Zeilah,
from jazzy Mogadiscio and from the quiet hidden
valleys of the hills. There was even a small contingent
from Ethiopia and another from Aden. All kinds of
girls—girls tall and lithe, girls buxom and short, girls
with copper skins and girls with skins as dark and soft
as the night sky, girls who walked stately as ancient
Egyptian queens, girls who jostled and tittered, shy
girls with the veil of purdah over their faces, bold
girls with no headscarves, girls with the eyes of gazelles and girls with the voices of vixens, girls who
were there out of compassion and girls who were
there out of curiosity.

The parade assembled outside Elmii Bonderii's hut
on the appointed day. One by one, the girls were
ushered into the presence of the poet. Some of them
were so moved that they even bared their breasts, and

considering the modesty of strict Muslims, this speaks
a good deal for Elmii's appeal.

Did any of them catch his eye? They most em-
phatically did not. Out of love for Hodan, or out of
his sense of style, or perhaps both, Elmii Bonderii
remained true to the classic plot of his own story.

> If one beholds beauty, if ever a human can be satisfied,
> I have seen Hodan.
> Oh girls, you have touched the wound I was trying
>   to heal.
> Cover your breasts.

What about Hodan all this time? How did she feel?
She had never exchanged more than a dozen words
with Elmii. She had not even seen him more than a
few times, and she certainly had never been in love
with him. She was content to be the wife of Mohamed
the Leopard. It came as a shock to her to find herself
a public figure, and she was confused by the violent
persistence of Elmii's unaccountable love for her. She
grew more and more troubled, and finally she asked
her husband if she might go and see Elmii, only once
and only for a moment, in the hope that this might
console him. Mohamed Shabel gave his consent.

When Hodan arrived at the poet's hut in the early
afternoon, he had a high fever and had fallen asleep.
She waited beside his bed as long as she dared, but he
did not waken. When Elmii woke up at last, she was
gone.

> Ill-starred and evil it is, to sleep in the day!
> Do I bear a curse, that I should be denied the sight of
>   her?

He never saw Hodan again, for he died shortly afterward. He had known very little about her, and possibly that is just as well. What she may have been like, in reality, does not matter so much. She was the beloved person to Elmii Bonderii, the one who enabled him to find within himself the poetry he had not known was there.

Elmii Bonderii's reputation is still so strong in his own land that people often refer to him as the Prophet of Love. And although they are not supposed to, for it is blasphemous to speak in this way except of the religious prophets, young Somalis who are in love themselves will sometimes give him a true prophet's status by adding, whenever they mention him, "On his name be Peace."

NOTE: Lines from the *gabay* by Elmii Bonderii were translated by B. W. Andrzejewski, School of Oriental and African Studies, University of London. Lines by Salaan Arrabey are from a *gabay* translated by B. W. Andrzejewski, Musa Galaal and Margaret Laurence. Lines by Mahammed 'Abdille Hasan and by Abdillaahi Muuse were translated by B. W. Andrzejewski and I. M. Lewis and are from their book *Somali Poetry: An Introduction,* Oxford: Clarendon Press, 1964.

This article and the next were written in 1967, on commission for a magazine. I read vastly beforehand, and my children and I went to Egypt for a month, from mid-December 1966 until mid-January 1967. I wrote the articles upon our return to England. They were accepted by the magazine. Then came the Seven Day War. Tourism in Egypt suddenly became a thing of the past and the articles were not published. They seem now to have taken place in some other and distant world. I do not know what happened to Hanafy Bashir. I hope he has survived.

Good Morning to the Grandson of Ramesses the Second

The deep pink façade sprouts tropically with balconies and with bulbous urns bearing spikey anonymous greenery. There is a revolving door, but one is not permitted to revolve it personally. My two children and I are zoomed lightly through by one of the hotel porters, clad in scarlet cummerbund, white voluminous pantaloons and an embroidered jacket flamboyant as a red and yellow canna lily. He looks like a splendid figment of the imagination, and in a sense that is just what he is. To enter the Old Winter Palace, in Luxor, is to enter a fantasy, one of the two which dominate this place, for Luxor is immersed in two myths and quite literally nourished by two pasts. Ranking first, of course, is the unimaginably distant past of ancient Egypt. The other—to which this hotel salaams—is a more recent past, the end of the last century and the beginning of this, when Luxor was a fashionable wintering place for those of Europe's wealthy who liked to potter comfortably around temples in a near-perfect climate and perhaps employ an archaeologist or two to see what treasures the reluctant tombs might yield.

Inside the Persian-carpeted rotunda, a staircase with fancy wrought-iron railing curves upward with infinite gentleness, so as not to disturb the lengthy delicate gowns of ladies no longer with us. Nowadays, girls in slacks sprint the tiny steps three at a time. Everywhere there is mightily polished brass and mahogany that glows like dark red glass. I cannot understand why I should find the ghosts here so appealing, but I do. I even manage to convince myself that we are inhabiting, more than likely, the very same rooms used by Lord Carnarvon in 1922 when he and Howard Carter sensationally opened the tomb of Tutankhamun in the Valley of the Kings. Later, however, my passion for re-creating the past has a sensible restraint placed upon it, when I discover that Lord Carnarvon didn't in fact stay here at all. He had his own houseboat. I might have guessed.

The bedrooms are pure Edwardian. Above each ornate brass bed hangs a mosquito net edged with starched lace frills. The fireplace is marble-topped. One wonders what possible use a fireplace would be here. The drapes are weighty turquoise and gold brocade, and although a male guest would not find a plug for his electric shaver, he would discover in the bathroom a dandy hook for attaching his razor strop.

"Nileside," the porter says with a giftful gesture, as though offering us the fruits of paradise. "Your rooms are Nileside."

Next morning early, I can see what he meant. The brown river, with the sun rising, is momentarily golden as a pharaoh's accoutrement. The few feluccas with their sails spread to the light wind cause hardly more than a flutter on the water's even surface. The hills are there twice—once in the river, wavering and pale, and beyond the river their reality, the rose-beige rock of the sacred hills where the dead god-kings were taken to await their awakening on the other side of life.

Nileside. The word might be used to describe the whole of Egypt, for the river has always been the land's lifeblood. Especially here in Upper Egypt one realizes it. Luxor, six hundred miles from Cairo, exists upon a fertile strip which from a plane looks like a perilously thin green ribbon. The rest is desert.

Luxor is small now, but once it was the centre of the known world, in the days when it was called No-Amun, some four thousand years ago. Thebes (the name given later by the Greeks) became the capital of all Egypt, reaching its zenith with the 18th, 19th and 20th dynasties, about 1550 to 1090 B.C. The ram-headed Theban god, Amun, became as mighty as Re the sun god, and the two merged. As Amun-Re, the god was served by a huge priesthood whose affluence and influence nearly equalled those of the pharaohs themselves. Thebes became enormously rich. The wealth of Nubia and the Sudan poured in here—fine granite, aromatic gums, ostrich feathers, gold in phenomenal quantity, and an unending supply of slaves to be temple builders for the insatiable pharaohs. But the days of greatness could not last. They never do. Thebes declined as its rulers declined in their grasp of events, until finally it was burned by invading Assyrians.

By Greek and Roman times, the tourist trade had

already begun, and enthusiastic centurions (who seem by Egypt's standards almost like close contemporaries of ours) slithered into tombs and scrambled through broken temples, leaving their scratched names on the stones. In the Middle Ages the local *fellahin* worked up quite a brisk little business in the sale of distant forefathers, for European doctors then had considerable faith in the medicinal properties of well-decayed and nicely time-blackened Egyptian mummies, ground up and mixed with oil, as a treatment for pleurisy.

Modern Egyptology really began only with Napoleon's brief Egyptian conquest in 1798 and the discovery of the Rosetta Stone on which the same passage was carved in Greek as well as in the hieroglyphic and the demotic or shortened forms of writing the ancient Egyptian language. When Young and Champollion finally cracked the secret of the hieroglyphics, in the early 1800's, the inscribed walls of temples and tombs could at last speak. The deciphering of the ancient writing, the clearing of temples half buried in sand, the rediscovery of tombs, the slow piecing together of scraps of information—all this has been done by large numbers of devoted archaeologists and philologists, mainly in this century. Yet even now we know only a fragment of what must once have existed. As an eminent Egyptologist, the late Sir Alan Gardiner, once cautioned, "We are dealing with a civilization thousands of years old and one of which only tiny remnants have survived. What is proudly advertised as Egyptian history is merely a collection of rags and tatters."

If Karnak temple is only a rag and a tatter, the imagination becomes paralyzed at the attempt to picture what once stood here. We drive out from Luxor in one of the little horse-drawn carriages that are generally used instead of cars—another bit of the Edwardian fantasy. Accompanying us is our guardian angel and mentor, Hanafy Bashir. About thirty, slender and quick, Mr. Bashir has an earnest and rather anxious look except when he is smiling, when he radiates warmth towards all the world. He is Inspector of Guides, Public Relations man, and second-in-command at the local State Tourist Office. He also modestly describes himself as "the King of Luxor and the grandson of Ramesses ii." His greeting is always "Good morning," for the morning, he says, is a hopeful time, a time of promise. It is not lucky to say "Good evening" or "Good night." He shouts companionably to everyone as we jolt along avenues of willowy pepper trees and scarlet poinsettias with their petal-like leaves, past mudbrick dwellings painted blue or yellow, where children in long robes dash out to yell beggingly for small coins and break into titters as Mr. Bashir scolds them unseriously in Arabic.

Then we are there, at the largest temple in the world, called in the long days of its life "The Most Perfect of Places," for here dwelt Amun-Re, king of gods. Generation after generation of pharaohs added temples and chapels and halls and obelisks to Karnak, towards the greater glory not only of Amun-Re but also of themselves, for here they placed their likenesses in massive granite and here they caused to be carved with suitable exaggeration their boasts of battle, their accounts of plunder. I used to think that nothing could more blatantly combine the things of Caesar and the things of God than the patriotic statuary that clutters

Westminster Abbey, but at Karnak I can see that the British Raj even in its palmiest days was positively self-effacing compared with the pharaohs.

Karnak temple once covered four hundred acres. Even now, it could contain with ease ten European cathedrals the size of Notre Dame. The French scholar Champollion said of Karnak's builders, "They conceived like men a hundred feet high." This is true, but it does not endear them to me. They must have rejected their own frail humanity utterly, for they strove to be supermen. Yet in a way this is an unfair assessment of the pharaohs. They were sacred kings. They were believed to possess vast spiritual powers which could affect for good or ill the entire land, the entire people. They were believed to be gods—and so they believed themselves to be gods. The role of a god-man is to be compelled to act the part; his terrifying fate is to believe in it. No men in human history could less have avoided *hubris* or the sin of spiritual pride than these kings of ancient Egypt. It was born in them, demanded of them. And here at Karnak are their souls recorded in stone, a record both impressive and horrifying.

The walls of Amun-Re's great temple are sharp-lined, severe, and everywhere deeply carved with both hieroglyphics and pictures. Here is Ramesses II, eternally fighting the battle of Kadesh, his chariot horses rearing wildly, the lithe and giant king slaying multitudes of his enemies, who are portrayed in midget size. Here are the exploits of Sethi I and the greatest of warriors, Tuthmosis III. King after king celebrates the true object of his heart's worship—power.

It is the incredible Hypostyle Hall which most

stuns the mind. Perhaps it is too big, too overwhelming. One cannot cope with it. Covering an area of some 54,000 square feet, it contains 134 massive columns, all closely inscribed. I have read translations of hieroglyphic snatches, and the theme is always the same—"Look at me; I am the Greatest; I have built higher, have killed more, am more feared than anyone." These mammoth columns make me feel obscurely angry. At the same time, I recognize that they have a kind of violent appeal, an appeal to the violence that exists somewhere inside every skull, and is to be resisted.

In the temple of Ptah at Karnak there is a windowless and utterly dark shrine which is frightening in another way. The old man who guards the shrine lights a candle, and there—quite suddenly, in front of my face—is the sinister black granite face of Sekhmet, lion-headed goddess of war. I do not like the look of this goddess one little bit. My abhorrence of superstition is severely threatened. I would not come here alone at night for any money. Later I discover that the local population believes this statue to possess an evil spirit.

The sacred lake of Karnak has an entirely different atmosphere from the enclosed temples. Here, the sunlight is in command and the swallows swoop and hover low over the pool where once the sacred boats were ritually sailed at the times of festival to symbolize the cycle of the sun, for the god each night had to sail perilously through the underworld before the dawn could be achieved. A party of Egyptian schoolboys arrives, large seventeen-year-olds in grey slacks and sweaters. They pose for each other's cameras.

Beside a rose-granite giant scarab, one handsome boy strikes an attitude, looking as though he were a young king beside a temple of his own designing. Then they flash off again, shepherded by brave teachers, off to become acquainted, at least a little, with their own long long history.

"Come," Mr. Bashir says, with the look of someone who has saved the best until last. "We must now go and say good morning to my favourite queen."

There she is, in the forecourt of the great temple, standing diminutive and perfectly poised at the feet of her colossal lord, Ramesses II. The Queen Nefertari. I ask Mr. Bashir why she is his favourite queen. Why not Nefertiti, the wife of pharaoh Akhnaten, perhaps the most beautiful woman who ever lived? No, Mr. Bashir tells me. He prefers Nefertari because she is intelligent but not *too* intelligent, beautiful but not *too* beautiful, and because she has a gentle face.

In Luxor one is always having to make the mental shift between the world of the living and the world of the dead. Sometimes the present seems tawdry in comparison with the past, and yet it is a relief to come back, for living disorder is better than dead order. It is Ramadan, and those who are devout Muslims do not eat or drink anything from sunrise to sunset. As soon as the evening gun has sounded, however, the town rouses itself from its daytime torpor and launches into a night of frenetic activity. The shops of the town are dimly lighted holes in the wall, but all are filled with a vividness of voices. Shoemakers, brass sellers, tailors, perfume vendors—all shriek their wares' superior qualities. We stop and watch a man making *konafa*, wheaten batter sprayed on a huge hot griddle. When it is done, it looks like loops of fine spaghetti and is used for making a confection with nuts and sugar.

At a sidewalk cafe, musicians in long blue robes and turbans are playing drums and flutes. The music is raucous, minor-key, lively. A boatman breezes in, plunks down a few coins in front of the musicians and then, cane in hand, goes into a frenzied dance, all alone. The music seizes him. He becomes possessed, bending backwards until his head nearly touches the earth. When the dance is finished, he abruptly vanishes among the acacia trees that line the street, back to his boat, not waiting for comment or applause.

At the tourist end of the town, where the hotels stand beside the river, the souvenir shops stay open half the night. "No charge for looking!" is the cry. Some sell the ordinary conglomeration of inlaid boxes, leather bags, alabaster vases, blue scarab rings, ashtrays decorated with distorted versions of Queen Nefertiti's face. Others are "Dealers in Genuine Antiquities," and it is these which fascinate me, for the Luxor dealers have carried on a trade in new antiques since the 1860's. I am prepared to believe that genuinely old objects might possibly be found here from time to time, but most of the statuettes, the small funerary figures, the broken jars, the pieces of bronze suspiciously time-eaten and covered with what I can only think of as instant verdigris, these are, in Mr. Bashir's phrase, "very old—two hundred minutes ago." Yet there is a curious pleasure in sifting through all this junk, in shops where the incense smoulders fragrantly and where grotesque decorations such as a large and elderly stuffed crocodile are dotted about to give the place allure.

The midnight streets are growing quiet and the carriage horses' hooves are taking on a slower rhythm. The moon illuminates the sacred mountain as though from within, like an alabaster lamp. By the river's edge the houseboats and steamers sway and creak. Here are the classy floating Hiltons, the *Isis* and *Osiris*, and here the big old sternwheelers *Sudan* and *Memphis*. There is the little *Lotus* and the *Nile Express*. Possibly the most interesting is the regal *Kassed Kheir*, which once belonged to King Farouk. It still bears his crown and crest, no doubt left there in irony. "*We* own it now," Mr. Bashir says, reminding me that Luxor lives a present-day, not only two pasts, an immediacy whose conflicting aspects are expressed in the slogans I noticed in a local secondary school. One was vehemently nationalist, and proclaimed that THE ARAB REVOLUTION WILL FULFIL ITS OBJECTIVES AND DESTROY ITS ENEMIES. The other spoke not of swords but of ploughshares—THE KEY TO PROGRESS IS HUMAN ENDEAVOUR. After dormant centuries, building on a pharaonic scale is again taking place in the land, but with a different emphasis. Not so far upriver, at Aswan, is the immense and nearly completed High Dam, which will bring electricity to the villages the whole length of the Nile valley and will channel for the first time in history the spate of the great river itself, changing its annual flooding into controlled irrigation. One can only hope that the old pharaonic urge to extend boundaries will be allowed to die, leaving human endeavour to do what can and must be done here.

Luxor Temple, within the town, must surely have housed more gods than any other temple in the world. All the ancient Egyptian gods received homage here, and never have any people acknowledged more gods

—Amun-Re, king of gods; Mut, his wife; Hathor, the cow-headed goddess of love; Thoth, the ibis-headed god of wisdom; Horus, the falcon god, emblem of kingly power; Osiris, judge of dead souls; Isis, sister-wife of Osiris; the malevolent-faced Sekhmet, goddess of war; Anubis, the jackal-headed god of the cemetery and embalming; and a host of others. After the last pharaonic dynasty had died, the Greek and Roman gods were worshipped here. Later, the Coptic Christians used the place as a church, and their frescoes still cling in shreds to a few walls. After Islam became dominant, the mosque of Abu Hagaq was built around the columns of part of the temple, at a time when only the top of the colonnades showed above the sand. When the ancient temple was unearthed and partially restored, the mosque was left undisturbed and so it remains, on a second level, with the temple columns sprouting beneath its feet. We go inside the mosque, taking off our shoes. An old man is sitting cross-legged on the green carpet, reading the Qoran aloud in a low chanting voice. At the top of a narrow winding stair, we emerge onto the balcony of the minaret, where the *muezzin* calls the People of the Book to prayer at the appointed times, and from here we can see the whole of Luxor temple, the layers of its religions.

"This is not like Karnak," Mr. Bashir says. "This is a *really* holy place."

Men have believed so, for more than three thousand years. There is no God but God, the Muslims say. But they also say that Allah possesses ninety-nine names.

On the west bank of the river lie not only the tombs but also the mortuary temples, for the souls of departed kings had to be tended lest they die a second and irrevocable death in the other world. Each time my children and I, accompanied by Mr. Bashir, join the other tourists and cross the Nile to the necropolis, the same pattern emerges. We start out gaily as a flock of pigeons in the early morning, winging our way to the ferry boat, frantically eager to behold marvels, certain we can absorb half of ancient history in a day and still have time for lunch. In the evenings, returning, we are humbler. If we studied assiduously for our whole life-span, we would not comprehend half the story contained within the Theban hills. We are doomed to ignorance, and besides, our feet hurt. Mr. Bashir reacts otherwise. His confidence never ebbs and neither does his energy. He is keeping Ramadan, but despite the lack of food and water, he leaps lightly from stone to stone in innumerable temples and is quite capable of asking seriously who will race him to the next tomb. There are seldom any takers.

Queen Hatshepsut must have rivalled any of the pharaohs in the attempt to be a full-fledged god. Looking at her temple at Deir El Bahri, one feels that she had a gargantuan nerve to build here at all, for the brownish gold mountain rises behind the man-made structure in a semi-circle of sheer cliffs, a temple built by the gods themselves. But Hatshepsut was not one to be deterred either by gods or men. I wish it were possible to like her, this rare female pharaoh, but the personality that emerges from the stones is somewhat less than lovable. After the death of her first husband, Tuthmosis II, she married her step-son, Tuthmosis III, but took full power and reigned herself as pharaoh. She wore men's clothes and, more eccentrically, a false beard. She was totally egocentric, like most of the pharaohs. One inscription in her mortuary temple says "Her majesty became more important than anyone else. What was within her was godlike; godlike was everything she did." When she died at last (perhaps from being poisoned), Tuthmosis III took a vicious revenge. His workmen hacked away the queen's names and portraits everywhere. Undoubtedly he had been provoked greatly, but there is still something shocking, even today, about the sight of these defaced carvings, especially when one considers that the motive was not only to remove the queen from human memory but also to destroy her spirit in the other world.

"We call him the Jealous Boy," Mr. Bashir murmurs.

Hatshepsut's ships journeyed to what is now the Somali Republic, and in her temple the expedition is described in wall carvings. Here are the fish of the Red Sea, and here the ships setting out. Here they are trading with the inhabitants of the land of Punt, carrying aboard the boats such items as small trees packed carefully in baskets and intended as exotic additions to the queen's gardens. Some of the colours remain—orange, gold, soft green, turquoise, crimson. The details of this voyage convey a sense of humanity missing from most of the royal monuments, and one hopes that there may have been another side to the queen's character, after all.

All that remain of the mortuary temple of Amenophis III, builder of Luxor temple and father of the heretic pharaoh Akhnaten, are the two statues given the name of the Colossi of Memnon by the Greeks, who couldn't seem to pronounce Amenophis. Standing alone on a plain, they are much damaged but strangely impressive. One of them was said by Greek and Roman tourists to make a whistling sound at dawn. "Dew? Wind? Something like that," Mr. Bashir says vaguely. But the musical statue fell in an earthquake in 27 B.C., and when it was righted, the singing had disappeared. The real reason I want to see these statues is because Rimbaud carved his name on one of them. But all I can find, besides the Greek and Roman graffiti, is *W. Boggie, 1820.*

The great mortuary temple of Ramesses III, at Medinet Habu, does not resemble a temple at all. It looks like a fortress. A 20th Dynasty king, Ramesses III reigned for thirty-one years and carried his campaigns into Libya and Syria. His temple shows him to be a man obsessed with war. The battle scenes, cut ferociously deep into the stone, are everywhere, as is the king, a god-sized warrior, his bow in his hands, dominating both his own forces and the enemy. The severed hands of those killed by the pharaoh's soldiers are being counted and the numbers recorded by scribes. Some of the warriors, Mr. Bashir informs me, cheated and brought back women's hands, after which the king made a decree—no more hands. "He told them," Mr. Bashir says delicately, "to bring some other." In later times, Coptic Christians once lived in some of the chambers of the deserted temple. One wonders how they could have borne to live with the scenes of slaughter on every side. "It would be noisy here at night," Mr. Bashir observes, and I agree. It is easy to imagine the warlike spirits forever clashing, never able to cease.

But of all the pharaohs in the Theban dynasties, Ramesses II is the most useful. There were many pharaohs by the name of Ramesses, but there is a simple solution to the problem of determining exactly which one it was who erected this statue or built that temple: when in doubt, say Ramesses II. This helpful maxim is followed by guides and tourists alike. Even after more than three thousand years, the most loudly self-trumpeting pharaoh of them all has a way of imposing his infuriatingly haughty personality. His colossi are to be found at Karnak and Luxor and many other places, for no man has ever been fonder of his own image. At the Ramesseum, his mortuary temple, lies the broken statue of him, the statue that is said to have been the largest ever carved. Hewn of one piece of Aswan granite, it is reckoned to have weighed over a thousand tons. Now it is fragmented but its size can be guessed from the size of the ear—three and a half feet in length. One of the names of Ramesses II was Ozymandias, and it was this statue Shelley was talking about in the poem "Ozymandias." Shelley had not personally seen Egypt, and that "traveller from an antique land" who told the tale got a few details wrong. "Nothing beside remains" is carrying poetic licence a shade too far, and "The lone and level sands" don't in fact "stretch far away" at all. Nevertheless, standing here beside the fragmented giant, one feels that the arrogance and pride of Ramesses was perfectly expressed in the lines " 'My name is Ozymandias, king of kings: Look on my works, ye Mighty, and despair!' " And yet, are we justified in thinking that we can perceive the historical irony of Ramesses II, whereas the king himself could not? Perhaps he could not, consciously. But is there not something sadly desperate and fear-filled about all this profusion of statuary, all this compulsive repetition of his own face and body, exaggerated to these proportions? Perhaps Ramesses II believed in his own powers not more than most kings, but considerably less so. Possibly only Nefertari, she of the obligingly reassuring face, ever really knew.

The nobles were able to be more demonstrably human. Where the tombs of the kings portray only the relationship with the gods and where the temples record conquests until the air still seems shrill with them, the tombs of the nobles are altogether different, for the paintings there are scenes of everyday life, intended not for decoration but in order that the dead occupant might find the same amenities in his new spirit life. Here in the tomb of the Vizier Nakht, three girl musicians with elaborately elegant coiffures and come-on eyes are entertaining the guests at a banquet. In Vizier Ramose's tomb another banquet proceeds, and the faces of the host and his wife have a quiet assurance, almost a radiance. The tomb of Rekhmire, vizier under two pharaohs of the 18th Dynasty, tells the most of all, for here in perfectly preserved murals are people making wine, cleaning and trussing ducks, carving statues, making furniture, and here is the dignified but paunchy Rekhmire himself, performing all his official tasks, receiving offerings from his children, being given gifts from far countries—a giraffe, a cheetah, a dog-faced baboon, Syrian horses, tusks of ivory. Because the tomb of Sennufer, superintendent of the granaries, is cut deeply into the hill, the colours are still fresh. Time takes on odd and unnerving proportions in this tomb. It is impossible for me to realize that the artists who painted the ceiling like an arbour, with leaves and bunches of purple grapes, did not do so the day before yesterday. Has Sennufer actually been dead so long? Is he in fact dead at all? Then, mercifully, we are back in the dry noon air of reality, and just in time, before incurable enchantment has set in.

The villages along both sides of the river are surrounded with fields of onions and beans and sugar cane. Camels or water buffalo plod dispiritedly in never-ending circles, turning the water wheels. Donkeys trot along the dusty roads, and always there is the gaggle of children, and the women robed in black, carrying water jars on their heads. There is a school in nearly every village nowadays, and soon the power from the High Dam at Aswan will provide light after sundown. Things are definitely not the same as they were long ago. And yet—the donkeys along the road are exactly the same as the one in Hatshepsut's temple, and beside the river a luminous green-gold bird appears, looking as though it has just flown out of a painted scene in a noble's tomb. The ducks with shimmering blue heads could be the same ones as those being netted in the tomb of Nakht. And in the clear sky of dusk, a hawk flies very low, his wings the same shape as the sacred wings of the son of Isis and Osiris, like the god Horus still watching over the land.

The presence of the dead is continually felt, yet it does not depress the guides who must spend half their lives in tombs. Guides have changed a lot since the days when shoals of unschooled dragomen foisted their services upon tourists. The business is efficiently controlled by the government now. The new guides are required to take a three-year course, after secondary school, in which they study ancient and modern history, languages, hieroglyphics, and the art of the ancient, the Graeco-Roman, the Coptic, and the

Islamic periods. The government has allowed some of the old guides to remain, however, and while these men are not well educated, they have picked up a wide if sometimes garbled knowledge of their subject.

Aboudi is such a man. Nowadays he hires himself out by the trip on the tourist steamers that go between Luxor and Aswan. We meet him on the *Nile Express*, where in the warm clarity of the upper deck air I spend many hours watching the land slowly drifting by and thinking of those who have passed this way before. Along here in their barges floated generations of the pharaohs' armies and overseers, going upriver into Nubia for gold and slaves. On the river's banks the Roman legions marched when they took over Egypt after the collapse of the Ptolemaic dynasty with the death of Cleopatra. Here rode the horsemen who were the remnants of the Mamelukes' savage splendour, those strange blue-eyed Muslims, descendants of Caucasian slaves, who ruled Egypt for so long. They had already passed out of history, although they did not yet know it, when they fled this way in 1799, pursued by Napoleon's army. Here also came the Turkish and Albanian forces of Mohamed Ali Pasha, founder of the royal line of which King Farouk was the last. Slowly along this river, too slowly, came Wolseley's British soldiers in 1884, to relieve the siege of Khartoum, where General Gordon, hero or self-made martyr, was soon to be killed by the Mahdi's charging dervishes. But for Aboudi, none of this represents the true peaks of the past. The greatest, in his eyes, were the days of his young manhood, when he worked for Howard Carter, discoverer of Tutankhamun's tomb, the only royal tomb found intact with all its treasures.

"Ah," he says with pleasurable melancholy, "those were exciting times, by Jove!"

A mock sultan in a white fringed turban and a moss-green robe of fine wool, Aboudi is both a marvellous storyteller and an inveterate name-dropper, reeling off a list of the earls and duchesses he has guided through the Theban necropolis. He speaks with an exaggerated British-establishment accent, or rather a caricature of same, and he even possesses a clipped British-military moustache. Of all the tombs, he tells me, that of Tutankhamun is nearest his heart, for he was actually there when it was opened. All the old guides I have met were there in person on that momentous day in 1922. Carter and his patron, Lord Carnarvon, must hardly have had room to breathe. Never mind—undoubtedly some were actually there, and perhaps Aboudi was one.

In the Cairo Museum most of the treasures from the tomb can be seen today—the huge gold-covered shrines like a nest of boxes which housed the golden mummiform coffins; the incredible delicate gold death-mask of the boy-king; the gilded couches made in the form of leopards and mythical beasts; the throne with its intricate inlaid and affectionate picture of the pharaoh with his young wife; and, perhaps most moving of all, the ostrich-feather fan which for a little while when it was first discovered was light and graceful as new feathers until the outer air attacked it and forced upon it the fragility of its actual age. Tutankhamun was least important of pharaohs. He began his reign with the name of Tutankh*aten*, for he was the half-brother of Akhnaten, who is perhaps the most fascinating pharaoh to our contemporary minds, in that he was the only king in all the countless centuries who introduced monotheism, worship of the Aten, the Sun, and who for a short period defied Amun's powerful priesthood, moving his court to Amarna, where he died and his dreams with him. At Akhnaten's death, the priests of Amun once more became dominant; the boy-king's court was moved back to Thebes and his name changed to Tutankh-*amun*. His tomb is small, but he is one of the very few who still lie in the royal valley, for the sarcophagus remains in the tomb with the coffin containing the boy's body. The walls of the tiny chamber are covered with paintings of Tutankhamun being blessed by the gods, the scarlet and blue colours as strong-hued as they were when the brush strokes were placed there in 1339 B.C.

Aboudi gives me a blow-by-blow account of the tomb opening.

"Lord Carnarvon—he always smoked a cigarette in a long holder, you know—he said to Carter, 'Well, you *are* a lucky boy!' And when Carter first went in, he said, 'Dear me! Where is the mummy?'"

What difference does it make whether all this is fabrication or not? Aboudi brings that day alive for me.

He has, predictably, very little use for the new guides, who may know all the facts, but not, he believes, how to present them entertainingly.

"They say, 'This is a tomb of 18th Dynasty, King So-and-So, on and on and on,' and everybody goes to sleep."

His evaluation is understandable but not quite accurate. I cannot imagine anyone going to sleep while Mr. Negib is talking. He is one of the new school. He worked for fourteen years as a clerk in the Department of Antiquities and became so interested that he took the course and gained his guide's diploma. Tall and extremely handsome in a Nasser-like way, he wears a natty grey suit with a maroon plaid scarf tossed jauntily over a shoulder. He carries an ebony cane which he uses like a teacher's pointer, and he handles his group like pupils who are being taken into his confidence.

"Now you tell me—I forget—which king belongs to this tomb?"

And they chorus with obedient and delighted voices, "Tut-ankh-amun!"

In the tomb of Amenophis ii, the spiel is interrupted by a bewildered lady.

"Say, how come they buried some kings in the pyramids and some in this valley?"

Mr. Negib, mildly chiding as a patient teacher might be with a student who hadn't done even a scrap of her homework, replies.

"Madam, madam, the pyramids are *Old* Kingdom, and the Valley of the Kings is *New* Kingdom."

"Oh yes," says the lady, with touching vagueness. "I see."

Mr. Negib does not permit himself even a slight sigh.

The tomb of Amenophis ii is the one in which a number of the royal mummies were found in 1898. They had been moved here in antiquity to keep them away from the tomb robbers, in the days when Thebes was no longer all-powerful and when the priests of Amun-Re were struggling with limited success to keep the sacred bodies of the god-men from being stripped of gold by human-type men whose need and greed overcame their terror at the thought of desecrating the divine.

"The mummies were moved to a safety place," Mr. Negib says. "Where was this safety place? This same tomb we are looking at now."

The paintings are in austere black and red on a white limestone background, gods such as jackal-headed Anubis, guardian of tombs, with his sleek head and eerily listening ears. Mr. Negib, good Muslim that he is, is careful to point out that the ancient gods were imaginary gods. The tomb is very deep; the air is close and tepid. Mr. Negib escorts us out before we begin to feel too claustrophobic, but not before he has pointed out to the camera enthusiasts where best they can achieve good shots.

Doesn't he ever become bored, I ask Mr. Negib later, with repeating the same facts over and over, the same talk every day? No, he says, because he doesn't give the same talk every day. Some tourists want a great deal of background, while others want only a surface glimpse. The trick in being a guide is to be able to judge the general character of any particular group. Another quality a good guide should have—the ability to acknowledge that he doesn't necessarily have an answer.

"We are not Egyptologists—we must never forget that."

All the same, I have the impression that if ever he should find himself short on facts, he could confidently fall back upon charm. He examines my scarab ring to see if it is a good one, and finds that it clearly is not.

"Your ring is not valuable," Mr. Negib says. "Rather, the hand that wears it."

All around the nobles' tombs on the bleak rock of the sacred hills, and down as far as the green land that edges the Nile, live the people of Qurna, who are believed to be the direct descendants of the ancient Egyptians. Their ancestors were the workmen and artisans who fashioned the pharaohs' tombs, made funerary furniture and sarcophagi, and who also (for they knew the tombs like their own hands) formed the gangs of tomb robbers.

They are Muslims now, of course, and have been so for centuries, but nevertheless when a cache of newly discovered royal mummies was taken away from here in 1881 to be stored in the Cairo Museum, the *fellahin* of Qurna gathered along the Nile and wailingly mourned, the women loosing their hair in the old way, mourned because their dead and holy kings were being taken from them.

Throughout the centuries, the villagers have continued to carve the sandstone and white alabaster of the mountain. Many of the "genuine antiquities" sold in Luxor are their work, although they have lost the fine skill of their ancestors and nowadays cater to a mass market. These unique people have never forgotten their age-old art of grave robbery, either. They became such a nuisance with their surreptitious digging that the government a few years ago decided to move them away from the tombs. A new Qurna was built at a safer distance, neat streets and whitewashed houses. The new village stands almost empty beside the river today. The inhabitants of old Qurna simply refused to move. Most of them remain where their people have dwelt these four thousand years, beside the tombs on the hills.

The mudbrick huts are poor. In an upper room of

one, a coloured picture of Nasser shares wallspace with an Egyptian film actress. In the courtyard, children with eyes scarcely less veiled than the eyes of adults tend the waterwheel with its strapped-on earthen pots dipping perpetually into the deep well. A jaded-looking camel with open sores on its flanks plods unceasingly to turn the notched wooden circle. But poverty and pride co-exist. Leaving, I face the familiar problem of whether or not to proffer money. I am, after all, unknown and have intruded into their home. I hold the note unobtrusively in my hand and turn to Mr. Bashir for advice. He mutters through his teeth, "Give it to any child," and turns away in order not to witness my embarrassment, or to conceal his own. I give the offensive but welcome piastres to a young son of the house, who gravely stashes it away—his father can collect it from him later.

At the rim of Qurna, away from the bare brown rock, down beside the river-given green, there is a small inn, frequented mainly by artists from Cairo. Here the date palms rise in living outspread fans against the sky, and the water buffalo stand black and massive. The portly pigeons naively cluster and are netted for the day's menu. We sit down to a lunch of roast pigeons and rice, delectably cool tomatoes, tea served in glasses with mint, and fresh faintly golden-coloured bread. We are the guests of Sheikh Aly Abderasoul, and this is a pleasurable privilege, for his family is a renowned one.

In 1817, when Belzoni discovered the tomb of Sethi I, Sheikh Aly's grandfather, then a boy, worked for the Italian. The sarcophagus was empty, but Belzoni managed to make the most of it, for he sold it to Sir John Soane, and it is still in the Soane Museum in

London. A legend arose in Qurna, however, that Belzoni was led to believe he had found the burial chamber, whereas the true resting-place of Sethi I lay still further inside the mountain. Sheikh Aly's grandfather maintained that he knew where.

The Abderasoul family came into the public eye over several other matters. Ahmed Abderasoul, Sheikh Aly's father, was the one who found in 1871 a cliff shaft which contained a cache of royal mummies, hidden there by priests in ancient times to save them from tomb robbers. The family did not reveal the find. They prudently smuggled out bits and pieces of funerary jewellery and statuettes, and sold them to the Luxor dealers. Finally in 1881 the authorities got wise to the game when they found that genuine (rather than "Genuine") antiques were coming on the market. The Abderasoul family was detected, and Ahmed was sadistically punished by the then Turkish governor of the province, by being flogged on the soles of his feet. One of Sheikh Aly's uncles was said (although nothing was ever proven) to have taken part in a spectacular robbery in 1901 in the newly discovered tomb of Amenophis II.

Sheikh Aly is a gaunt, fine-featured old man, wearing a stark black robe, a white turban and an air of imperturbable self-confidence. The secret of the tomb of Sethi I, he maintains, was passed on from his grandfather to his father and thence to him. In 1960, he finally persuaded the government to let him dig. He found a series of steps and then a blocked passage, and at this point the government, losing faith, told him to stop.

"Think of the gold in Tutankhamun's tomb," he broods, "and he was not even an important king. Sethi the First was a great king. How much more must there be in his tomb?"

The tomb of Sethi I is the largest in the valley. Sethi, who was the father of the self-adoring Ramesses II, restored the empire which had dwindled under the monotheistic pharaoh Akhenaten. The gorgeously walled tomb is covered with hieroglyphics and weird deities in meticulous relief, the scenes and inscriptions raised in stone and painted river-blue, sun-scarlet, gold, and a black which is still dark as the underworld. At the entrance, on the limestone facings, are inked-in sketches, the first step of work that was never completed. The artists seem close, certainly breathing, absent only momentarily. It is difficult to believe that the work was abandoned about 1291 B.C. when the pharaoh died.

The purpose of Sheikh Aly's life has become the attempt to convince the Department of Antiquities to let him probe further into Sethi's tomb, both for the sake of the treasure and in order to vindicate his family. He believes in his dream utterly. Some of the Luxor dealers believe otherwise.

"Sheikh Aly—"one of them says with a shrug. "The truth is that Sheikh Aly is mad."

Who really knows? I myself am prejudiced on Sheikh Aly's side for two reasons, neither remotely related to logic—his burning faith, and his frank acknowledgement of the world's ways and his own. He gives my young son a sandstone statue a foot high.

"Not antique, but in ten years it will be antique."

Perhaps in six months, I suggest.

"Certainly," Sheikh Aly says, his eyes gleaming with a hard humour. "Why not?"

A last view of the pharaonic past is Karnak Temple

at night. There are no other people here. Our footsteps sound louder than they are. The moonlight is phosphorescently apparent here where there are no artificial lights. In the Hypostyle Hall, the phantom priests forever tend their gods, and in a hundred chapels the rituals live again in shadow as they can no longer do in sunlight. A black shape slips around a column. It is a jackal, one of the many who still inhabit this place at night—Anubis remaining faithfully with the spirits of his dead kings. I find it reassuring to come back to the watchmen in the forecourt of Amun's great temple, the slight and living figures sitting around their small living fire.

I know quite well that it is useless to interpret the past through one's own concepts, just as it is useless to try to interpret oneself through these much-too-old stones. Yet I persistently keep trying to do both. Something about the magnificence and the futility of these structures, something about the tenacity and the ultimate vulnerability of the kings, men who built them in an attempt to defeat the undefeatables, time and death—this will haunt the mind always, as the jackals haunt the temples, for it contains all there is of human paradox.

But it is the living, in the end, whom one can see and speak with, even a little. When we arrive home from Egypt, there is a postcard waiting for us from Mr. Bashir. It says, in Arabic and English, three words. "Good morning, everyone."

This article seems especially strange, in an ironic way, because for years I felt that my final comment about the importance of the Suez Canal in its second century could scarcely have been more mistaken. Even though I read the English-language newspapers when I was in Egypt, I did not foresee the war with Israel. I could see Nasser's desire to be a twentieth-century pharaoh, as leader of the Pan-Arab world, of course, and I could see, as indicated in both the previous article and in this one, where such a desire might lead. I suppose I desperately wanted to believe, for the sake of the ordinary people on both sides, that the Arab states would come to realize the necessity of accepting Israel's ancestral right to be. The canal was closed for all the intervening years, but it did open again in 1975, so its second century may be of significance after all. One can only pray that such significance may become a peaceful one.

Captain Pilot Shawkat and Kipling's Ghost

A slender blue spear of water improbably piercing the desert. Unimposing to look at, tranquil, even drab, once you have become used to its presence there at all. Yet it is very much more than a place, and its meanings extend vastly beyond the function it serves. Variously, it has been an omen of imminent loneliness, an *esprit de corps*, a long sigh for the past or a prayer for the future. The pharaohs dreamed of it; a Frenchman was obsessed by it; ten thousand men died in its creation. A king once bartered it and a prime minister bought it. A colonel once vowed to blow it up, but an imported army prevented him. Half a century later, another and more confident colonel claimed and won it. Statesmen have wrangled and wrung their hands over it; it has extracted more than that from soldiers sent to attack or defend it. For most of its near-century of existence it symbolized and contributed to one way of life. Now it symbolizes and contributes to quite another. Few places in the world have been more emotionally loaded than the Suez Canal.

The car zips effortlessly along the excellent highway east from Cairo. On either side, the only visible life is an occasional lanky camel searching the sand for dry bluish thorn bushes which somehow nourish it. The driver's transistor radio gives forth with the raw grieving voice of Omo Kolsoum, a singer now in her sixties, who has been for many years as beloved in Egypt as Piaf was in France. Yet this is not Egypt, not any longer. It is the United Arab Republic. The name comes naturally enough to the tongue now. Whatever one's feelings about it—and my feelings, like many people's, tend to be mixed—it is an undeniable entity. Although the revolution took place in 1952, the long semi-colonial era of European influence really ended only in 1956 when Nasser took over the Suez Canal.

"Ship me somewheres east of Suez, where the best is like the worst"—Kipling's British tommy, off to Mandalay where life wasn't all fun and flying fishes, expresses definitively what Suez, at the southern end of the canal, used to be. For several generations of soldiers, tea-planters, and district officers, Suez was the last link with home before the beginning of an exile which was sometimes forced but perhaps more often self-imposed. The ship's emergence from the canal, on the voyage to the Far East, meant the final goodbye to England, goodbye to Mama or Mum, goodbye to tea on the lawn or a pint at the pub. From here on it would be gin and sweat, malaria and duty. The vestiges of this past still cling around Suez, but its significance today centres around the fact that it is the gateway to the oil of the Middle East, and at this point 75 per cent of all transiting goods on the canal are oil products.

British Traveller is a tanker steaming from the Persian Gulf with a cargo of crude oil. She is in the northbound convoy which will journey straight through the canal without stopping, while the two southbound convoys wait at Ballah By-Pass, Lake Imsah, or the Great Bitter Lakes, for these are the only three places where ships may pass. The northbound convoy is allowed precedence because so many of the ships are tankers, heavily laden, not easily manoeuvred, and carrying highly dangerous cargoes. The first thing that strikes me as we go aboard with the pilot is the profusion of No Smoking signs displayed on *British Traveller*'s decks, those grey metallic slabs dotted with scarlet or white valves leading to the inflammable black gold below.

The Captain is a soft-spoken Scot who says that the wife of one of the officers is aboard, and would I like to meet her. She is a thin and still-attractive woman in her forties. Her hands are faintly but unceasingly agitated, like the wings of evening moths. She has not, she tells me, spoken to another woman since they left Bombay, where they discharged their last cargo before reloading in the Gulf. She does not have children. She has "lived Tyneside" all her life. Now she comes to sea with her husband. The large cabin is chintzy, ornamented with bric-a-brac. She has put her mark upon it, but "it isn't like home, not really." She does tapestry in wools to pass the time, and a while ago she enjoyed visiting Australia because in Perth there was a park that was "almost like England." It would be wrong to feel sorry for her. She doesn't feel sorry for herself. She is not aware that she is a gallant lady.

On deck, I watch the sands slip by and experience a feeling of unreality—how can we be sailing through the desert? To starboard lies the Sinai desert, where Moses led the Children of Israel. An occasional billboard instructs us to buy DEWAR'S SCOTCH or to FLY BOAC. Parallel to the canal runs a small freshwater canal, here called "sweetwater," which makes it sound more appetizing than it looks. At intervals there are villages with eucalyptus trees, casuarina whose long drooping branches look as though they were hung with moss, date palms, mangoes, and the giant green hands of castor oil leaves. Water buffalo placidly feed among the clover, while black-swathed women of elegant posture carry huge clay water jars on their heads and still seem to walk lightly as birds.

Four pilots are needed to take any ship on its fifteen-hour trip through the canal—one to pilot the vessel into Suez harbour, one to take her from Suez to Ismailia halfway up the canal, another from Ismailia to Port Said, and a fourth to guide her out of Port Said harbour. Captain Pilot Shawkat Gemes is *British Traveller*'s pilot from Ismailia to Port Said. He is typical of the new school of pilots, and in many ways he represents part of the canal's new meaning, for the takeover of the canal and its subsequent efficient operation by Egyptians has had an enormous effect in establishing a national confidence. He is tall and broad, in his early forties, not actually handsome but with an attractively strong-boned face and a firm voice. He talks without ever taking his eyes from the narrow waterway, and from time to time he breaks off to give an order to the seaman at the helm: "Port ten—Midships—Starboard five." The vessel must be kept dead centre to allow maximum clearance of the canal bottom, for the water depth is greatest in the middle.

"This ship," he says, "being a tanker and heavily loaded, sits low in the water, so she is like an iceberg —most of what counts is underneath the surface. If she veers a fraction too much on either side, she could become uncontrollable. A ship of this size cannot be righted instantly. The thing is never to get yourself in that situation. I have to watch constantly, of course, but after you have taken hundreds of ships through, you can feel if your ship is veering. Also, you know the tendencies of any particular ship."

A file is kept, he tells me, of every ship transiting the canal, and relevant information is handed to a pilot before he embarks. "Does she tend to swing to starboard? Is she slow in responding to changes of course? The pilot must know all this in advance." The first time a ship goes through the canal, she must be accompanied by several tugs because her individual quirks are not yet known.

Captain Pilot Shawkat Gemes is very definite on the subject of the English and French pilots who walked out at the time of the Suez crisis in 1956.

"They were very proud men. Great snobs. They believed that if they left, the whole canal would fall to pieces. They deceived their governments, you know, by giving the impression that the canal couldn't operate without them. This was because they deceived themselves—they believed they were supermen."

He is harder on those pilots than he is on their governments. It is odd to hear the whole episode stated in such highly personalized terms, but possibly he resents those men with some justification, for before 1956 there were only thirty-one Egyptian pilots out of 187, and the Egyptians were not allowed to pilot the larger ships. Now most of the pilots are Egyptians —or rather, as they are known officially, Arabs. No British or French pilots are hired, but there is a sprinkling of other nationalities—Greek, Spanish, Norwegian, and one American.

"A pilot has to have his master's papers before he can begin training for canal service. Quite a few pilots, like myself, came from the Egyptian Navy when the canal was re-opened after the Suez war. Pilots had to be produced quickly, so each one was trained intensely on his own section. I trained on the section from Port Said to Ismailia, and worked here for several years without knowing one inch of the canal from Ismailia to Suez. Later, when the pressure was not so great, we went in small groups and learned the other sections."

When he says "the canal," he makes it sound like "The Canal," something more than a physical thing, an object of loyalty and even affection, the residence of a camaraderie which is not mentioned but can be distinctly felt.

Accidents on the Suez Canal are very infrequent, but a pilot does not have much margin for error. The greatest hazard in piloting is the water pressure created within the confined space of the canal by the movement of the big ships. This is a doubly threatening force, for it can cause a ship to carry on for a considerable time even if all engines are shut off, or it

120

can swivel a slightly off-course vessel until she slams into the canal sides. Pilots must keep ships rigidly on course and must adhere carefully to the speed limit and to the prescribed distance between ships. Timing is all-important, Captain Shawkat Gemes tells me. The southbound convoys must be at a by-pass at the proper time, and the northbound convoy must appear when expected. Movements of all ships are supervised and coordinated by the Canal Authority HQ at Ismailia.

One can see the grooves and hollows where the seemingly harmless ripples have scoured the canal banks. The Canal Authority has a fleet of dredgers which is kept constantly busy with canal repair. These unwieldy barges, heavy with cranes and chains, are used in canal improvement as well. In the last ten years the canal has been widened and deepened, and a five-year project has begun for further enlarging. *British Traveller* has a draught of thirty-four feet. The maximum draught which the canal will take at the moment is thirty-eight feet, but by 1968, a forty-foot draught should be possible.

At Ballah By-Pass the southbound convoy is waiting until our northbound convoy passes. We see them from a long way off, before we can see the water they sit in, so they look grotesquely beached, like great dead whales washed ashore or Noah's arks left perched on land after the floods receded. One of them, mysteriously, is carrying a load of red double-decker London buses. Why, and for whom? But we steam past, and cannot enquire.

Night comes suddenly, and for a while on deck there is only the darkness and the stars. Inside the bridge, the pilot's voice intermittently enters the silence—"Starboard ten—Midships—Port five." Then, ahead of us,

Port Said appears, the orange-coloured canal lights and the lighted streets shimmering in the black water like a second and surrealistic city.

On the dock, Captain Pilot Shawkat Gemes, nonchalant in beige pea-jacket, hands over his attaché case to a boy who has appeared from nowhere the instant we stepped ashore.

"See?" the pilot says with a pleased grin. "Timing."

Although the Suez Canal belongs to modern history, a vision of it began in pharaonic times. An ancient forerunner of the present canal was one originally built during the reign of Senoueret II, about 2000 B.C., and which linked a tributary of the Nile with the Red Sea. This canal was abandoned and then restored briefly, once under the Ptolemaic kings and again during the Roman and early Islamic eras. The redoubtable Queen Hatshepsut, who ruled as pharaoh in her own right, sent her ships by way of this canal, about 1495 B.C., on one of the world's first trade missions, to the east coast of Africa.

Seventeenth- and eighteenth-century French savants debated the possibility of a canal through the isthmus of Suez, but the prevailing (although mistaken) opinion for a long time was that such a canal could never be built because there was too great a disparity between the levels of the Red Sea and the Mediterranean. It was not until the appearance of Ferdinand de Lesseps that the canal became anything more than a subject of speculative talk. After de Lesseps was appointed French consul-general in Alexandria in 1835, he grew friendly with Mohamed Said, son of the Egyptian ruler, and perhaps even discussed with him the feasibility of a canal. In 1854, Mohamed Said became khedive. The nearly twenty years had not diminished de Lesseps' profound belief. He bustled off to Egypt at once and obtained from Mohamed Said a concession authorizing him to form the Compagnie Universelle du Canal Maritime de Suez. The company was to have the canal for ninety-nine years, after which the Egyptian government was to take control. Shares were sold, most of which went to the governments of France and Egypt. Britain opposed the scheme vigorously, even viciously, for she saw it, quite accurately, as a French bid for power in the East.

Begun in 1859, the canal took ten years to construct, and only de Lesseps' steel will kept things going. It was like a repetition of the pharaohs' monuments, appallingly paid for in human lives. The khedive contributed huge numbers of forced labourers, who died in droves, of cholera and of heat-exhaustion, working in the unrelieved desert under the hammer blows of the sun. Finally the gruelling job was completed, and the waters of the Mediterranean joined those of the Red Sea. The opening ceremony, on November 17, 1869, was lavish in the extreme. Five hundred chefs were brought from France, twenty military bands made loud the desert air, and the canal was mightily blessed by priests of the Roman, Greek, and Coptic churches as well as by imams of Islam. Innumerable festive cannon were fired as Empress Eugenie of France led the way in the royal yacht *Aigle* towards Ismailia, where the ships from Suez met those from Port Said, and everyone banqueted and danced all night under multitudinous lanterns, while the sky boomed and glittered with fireworks. One of the guests was Stanley, who was really interested only in going off to look for Livingstone, but who had been told by his boss on *The New York Herald* that he must attend the opening of the Suez Canal first.

Egypt did not benefit long from the canal. In 1875, the Khedive Ismail, pursuing a life of gaudy spending, discovered that he was bankrupt and his credit rating was nil. He therefore looked around for someone to buy Egypt's shares in the Suez Canal. He did not have to look far. Britain had undergone a decided change of heart about the canal, when she saw that it cut the journey from Europe to India in half, and that the Canal Company itself was likely to prove a highly profitable venture. Khedive Ismail had only to nod, and Disraeli snapped up what amounted to a controlling interest in the canal shares, for four million pounds sterling. Not surprisingly, the feckless Ismail was deposed in 1879, but like Farouk after him, he left the country in his royal yacht, no doubt comforted by the fortune in cash and baubles which accompanied him.

Britain by this time was dabbling pretty seriously in Egyptian affairs. The British and French consuls, between them, almost entirely directed the young Khedive Tewfik. But when a group of Egyptian army officers, led by Colonel Ahmed Arabi, marched to the palace in September 1881, and informed Tewfik that he was no longer king, the British government intervened decisively. The British Navy shelled Alexandria, and Colonel Arabi swore he would destroy the Suez Canal, which at this point must have seemed about as much use to Egypt as a plague of locusts. Britain grew increasingly alarmed about her investment and her shipping, and in 1882 General Wolseley was sent to Egypt with twenty thousand men. The canal was promptly occupied, the nationalists were ousted, and Arabi himself was exiled to Ceylon.

History may have the knack of repeating itself, but it always does so with variations which confuse even the wary. Colonel Gamal Abdel Nasser in 1956 may have seemed the same man as Arabi, but he was far from it. He was shrewder and more certain of himself, and he had been in power for several years. The whole tone of the country was quite different, as was the tone of the world in general. It was not to be the same easy and internationally accepted occupation of the canal by imperialist powers as it had been in 1882. The period Kipling had portrayed was all but dead; the European sahib had played his historical part, and the curtain was due to go up on the next act.

That small and shabby war, known elsewhere as the Suez Crisis, but usually called "The Aggression" by Egyptians, did not reflect much credit on either Britain or France—a point widely admitted today in both countries. On July 26, nationalization of the canal was announced by Nasser. The British and French pilots walked off in mid-September, and in October, British and French forces bombed Egyptian bases and invaded the canal zone. Fighting went on until early November, when the United Nations ordered Britain and France to withdraw, which they did. Today in Port Said there is a Martyrs' Square with a large grey granite obelisk commemorating those who died, but surprisingly little rancour seems to remain. "It was like any other war," a merchant says with a shrug. "People were killed, and it was hard to believe it was happening. But now—it is past."

What is remembered, though, is the way in which some thirty Egyptian pilots kept the canal operating, by themselves, after the departure of the British and French pilots, until it was closed by the fighting two months later. Captain Pilot Shawkat Gemes speaks of those men in the way that an Englishman might speak of the Battle of Britain pilots.

"Let me tell you—it was a fantastic thing they did. It was not any longer a job. It was a challenge. It was something they *had* to do, to prove that Egyptians could run the canal. A pilot would bring a ship all the way from Suez to Port Said—no relief pilot, no harbour pilots—and then he would turn around and take another on the southbound convoy. Maybe he would have one or two hours sleep before the next trip. But all the convoys got through, all of them, and on time."

Captain Pilot Mustapha Wahab is more restrained when he speaks of those days, for he was actually there. Now in his mid-fifties, he is sophisticated, tough, courteous, and the possessor of an undeceived eye. The exhaustion of those months is what he remembers most.

"It was fine at the beginning—you begin strongly, but like a long-distance runner you must have strength for later on, and at first we did not realize that. After three or four runs, with one pilot doing the job of four, we began to feel it. But we could not stop. It was—you might say—not just for ourselves."

At Ismailia, headquarters of the Suez Canal Authority, the emphasis is nearly all on the world of right-this-minute. Nearly, but not quite. Amid the purple bougainvillaea and the palms, at the curiously striped yellow and maroon Resthouse for important visitors, one room remains not so much a ghost but rather a cadaver of the past, for this house was once de Lesseps', and his bedroom has been preserved just as he left it. The sun-damaged bronze brocade drapes are frayed now, falling to pieces, and on the walls the French wallpaper with its blue and gold pattern is peeling in long shreds. The relics are oddly touching—a marble-topped washstand, pink china soap dishes, small medicine bottles, a blue glass decanter, the family Bible, a stilted photograph of de Lesseps and companions looking at once foolish and formidable in Bedouin dress. The dusty sense of a long yesterday is almost choking in here, and I am reminded of the old etchings in the Canal Authority offices, showing the canal being built—the gangs of spindly turbaned labourers, the balking camels, the incredibly frail and inadequate-looking equipment. It is understandable that Egyptians have split feelings towards de Lesseps, as they have always had towards the canal itself. They are gaining wealth from it now, but it has brought a lot of grief in the past. They will not restore this tiny museum, but they will not abolish it, either. They leave it untouched.

One wonders what de Lesseps would make of the canal these days. During the first year of its life, five hundred ships passed through. By 1913, the number had risen to more than five thousand a year. In 1965, the ships totalled more than twenty thousand a year. At the top of the Canal Authority's new white building in Ismailia, facing Lake Timsah, the Movements Room constitutes the nerve centre of the canal. Here, communication is maintained by direct line to the many signal posts along the canal, and each post reports on every ship as it passes. Fifty-seven ships a day, on an average, travel through, and a large proportion of these are oil tankers. As the flow of oil has increased from the Persian Gulf, the canal revenues have steadily mounted, and in the year 1965–66 these totalled the equivalent of $197 million. A problem which may ultimately become serious is the existence of the new supertankers, for it is not likely that the canal can ever be expanded enough to accommodate these ocean mammoths. Some oil companies are even now finding it cheaper to use fewer and larger tankers and to take them around the Cape.

When the canal was nationalized, Nasser announced his intention to use canal revenues to help finance industries and such large-scale projects as the Aswan High Dam. This he has done, although the dark side of the coin is the fact that canal resources have been increasingly dipped into for armaments. In the three canal towns, Port Said, Ismailia, and Suez, ship repair and building companies have been established under the auspices of the Canal Authority. Shipyards have been built at Port Fuad, opposite Port Said, and the harbour itself has new deep quays and a floating dock used for major ship repairs.

I first saw Port Said sixteen years ago. My memory presents me with the high-prowed and beautifully decorated dhows in the harbour, and the streets of closely huddled bazaars swarming with insistent con men determined to show visitors the sights, and gully-gully men who magically drew forth baby chicks from overturned cups which had been empty the moment before.

The land on which Port Said stands has grown since then, reclaimed from the sea, and new apartment blocks have grown with it. In the summer, tourists from Cairo inhabit the yellow stucco cabins which are peppered along the shore, and a government-owned luxury hotel is rising, although local inhabitants say it has been rising for so long they despair of its completion.

Along the waterfront and in the back streets, the old Port Said still reigns. Bazaars with names like Woolworth Exhibition or, outlandishly, Harry Lauder, display tawny white-streaked alabaster lamps and figurines which may not be plastic but look it, scarabs and inlaid boxes, carpets, and a dizzy array of jewellery both true and false. The Golden Scissors reassures the passer-by—YOU MAY HAVE CONFIDENCE IN ALL OUR DEALINGS. (You *may*, but if you do, you are probably pretty naive.) But the marks of change are to be seen even here. The squat solid Victorian office buildings draw their ornate wooden shutters against the noon sun, as always, but the brass plaques at their doors name British and French firms no longer here. A few Italian cafés remain, and a few Greek shops sell movie magazines and startling oil paintings of lurid landscapes or somebody's fantasy notion of a harem. Otherwise, the Greek and Italian communities, once sizable, have disappeared, owing chiefly, I am told, to their refusal to take on U.A.R. citizenship.

Simon Arzt department store was once famous as the supplier of imported goods to homesick Europeans who were finicky about obtaining the right brand of soap or tobacco. Now, in desperation (oh, ghostly memsahibs, shed a tear in your white heaven), it has begun to stock the same line of souvenirs as the Oriental Gift Shops, although it keeps a trace of its former tone by displaying these vulgar objects in high glassed-in mahogany cases. The gilt signs are like whispered runes, conjuring up another era— LADIES MANTLES—GENTS TROPICAL WEAR—and, with a picture of what used to be known as a Bombay bowler, ELWOOD'S HELMETS. Simon Arzt's Cigarettes still trumpets, albeit feebly, ROYAL DRAGOON—NO HALF AND HALF AFFAIR INDEED; A RIGHT-DOWN REGULAR ROYAL WEED. Upstairs, the plaster models of women with 1920 hairstyles are wearing garments of a mournful bagginess. Few clerks and fewer customers tiptoe around, and it is a relief to get outside and see on a roadside kiosk a copy of "Batman" in Arabic.

The reality of Port Said is the harbour, the shipyards, and the canal, a reality which no longer relates to a resident community of expatriates. Along the quay a rifle-bearing soldier paces out his boring guard duty, but otherwise there is little sign that this is a military zone, except for the U.A.R. gunboats which one morning flash about on manoeuvres. Across the harbour, the Port Fuad shipyards are completing two new freighters. At the water's edge, amid a pile of rubble near the shipyards, lies the bronze and now-green statue of Ferdinand de Lesseps, which was blasted from the harbour entrance. "He has been lying there for ten years," an Egyptian friend says. "He must be getting tired." But the canal builder was not consigned to permanent oblivion at the harbour bottom—that is the interesting thing. Ironically enough, not far away from the couchant de Lesseps stands a giant and presumably inspirational portrait of President Nasser.

Port Said harbour is loud with the ships of the world—freighters, tankers, passenger ships, some of them loading and unloading their cargoes, some waiting to go into the canal with the next convoy. Here is the freighter *Jalavishnu*, from Bombay, the tanker *British Ivy*, the Swedish freighter *Songhkla*, the Japanese *Nuseki Maru*, the huge Norwegian tanker *Berg*

Haven, the Greek *Frossini* from Piraeus, letting down anchor chains with earsplitting metallic groans. There is a constant to-ing and fro-ing of pilot launches, tugboats, and the small motor boats and rowboats which go out to help moor the ships. Cockleshells of green and white, painted sky-blue on the inside, bounce along the waves created by larger craft, on their way out to the anchored ships with crates of oranges, sandals, souvenirs. The activity never stops, for a port does not rest.

At the Casino Palace, oldest hotel in Port Said and at one time very classy, the past again nudges. If old soldiers never die but merely fade away, the same must be true of old hotels. Facing the harbour, its fissured yellow walls half hidden by an entanglement of palm and bougainvillaea and listless red hibiscus blossoms, the Casino Palace has an overwhelming air of decayed splendour. An outside pavilion retains its mosaic floor and its globed lights like four-leaf clovers with wrought-iron stems. Its roof is glass, high and sloping, like a Victorian railway station. In the heyday of the old Canal Company, the French and British used to come here to partake, so I am told, of teatime concerts as well as evenings of convivial waltzing. But now the bandstand is deserted, and the wicker chairs are rarely used except by an occasional Egyptian couple sipping Cokes. The dining room has a handwritten notice advertising an assortment of bewildering delicacies such as PIPSI COLA, SODA LARGE AVEC WHISKEY, CAFE THE SIMPLE, and CAFE THE CAKE OU TOAST, but a waiter says that the list refers only to the summer season, when "we have people from Cairo." In the lounges, armchairs are slip-covered in worn linen prints of English foxhunting, and in the billiard room the burly tables are perpetually shrouded in dustcloths. The halls contain Persian rugs, now trampled thin, and potted ferns in troughs plump with plaster cherubim. The place is almost empty except for an old woman with white hair and a death's-head face who paces the halls unceasingly. Is she an ex-countess? A deposed sovereign? A retired school-teacher? I dare not speak to her in case she dematerializes.

Abdul, the headwaiter, has been here for many years. I am impertinent enough to ask him what it was like when the hotel was being used as a billet for British officers during the Suez War. He smiles in polite rebuke to my question. "It is over," he says. He is pleased and excited at the moment, for the Greek passenger ship *Patris* is in: "Tonight we have three hundred and sixty for dinner." This does not happen so often any more. Later that evening, they gush into the dining room, overflow into the bar, examine chatteringly the souvenirs which have suddenly appeared in the main lobby, and generally impart a heartening life. But they are gone by ten-thirty, and once more the only sounds are the creaking and clanking of anchor chains and small floating iron piers in the harbour, and the muted footsteps of a steward in the old pavilion underneath my window, as he straightens the orange-painted tables and the wicker chairs, placing them back into a neatness that has become habitual.

This century returns with the arrival of the Wander-birds. "We're moored to that palm tree across the road," Cheryl tells me, and there it is—a beat-up American station wagon carefully roped to the tree in a hopeful gesture towards security.

"We just came into the hotel to use the bathroom," explains Cheryl, who is nineteen, Oregon-born, and pleasingly garrulous. "It's Dan's station wagon, and the other three boys and I just hitched up with him along the way. They look out for me, see?"

Cheryl is at once shy and brassy, tough and naive. The boys believe she is only a kid (for she looks younger than she is), never suspecting that they may be the same. Simon and Derek are English, both in their early twenties, both tightly encased in the convolutions of their own skulls. Dan is an American who would like to be a Mormon. He feels inadequate to the self-discipline expected, but he talks the new revelation constantly. "God as a man within our lifetime, see?" The Swede, Eric, is small and stocky, inclined to get into fights when drunk, but he is the one who is most consistently considerate towards Cheryl.

In the evenings, they liven the pavilion with earnest words. "Life, like, you know, must in some essential way be beyond destruction . . ." The country is full of them. Some of them hope to hitch their way down the east coast of Africa. They get as far as Egypt and discover they can't get visas for the Sudan and other African countries, because these governments not unnaturally want some assurance that travellers have enough money to get themselves home again. The British consul tells me gloomily about his problems with those who are his nationals. "Some of them think they can work their way, but all they can do is drive a truck, and most of the indigenous population can do that." The Egyptian government is fairly lenient and only forces drifting souls to drift a little further when they take to sleeping in public parks, or begging and thieving. The Wanderbirds haven't gone that far into need or despair, at least not yet. They talk, talk, talk. Do they actually *see* the harbour, the canal, the ships? Have they noticed that they are in Port Said? In some ways they seem inturned utterly. And yet there is a graveness and a searchingness about them. They are pilgrims who are not certain what pilgrimage they have undertaken. They do not know where their Mecca is, or even if there is a Mecca, but they are compelled to go on.

It is, of course, completely in the cards that the Wanderbirds should encounter the Sailor. In his mid-thirties, with a darkish beard, incongruous blond hair and narrow pained eyes, the Sailor is damaged in more ways than one. His surface hurt is due to the fact that he fell from a slipped plank to the steel wall of a bulkhead and cracked his back. He was put off ship here, hospitalized for a time, and now awaits a flight back to New York. At least, this is the story he gives me. The Wanderbirds receive a different one, with sensational hints of battle on a near-Homeric scale. It is interesting to get varying views. Seamen are in short supply these days, a member of the American consulate tells me, and shipping companies are apt to sign on anybody they can get. If a merchant ship has a young crew plus a couple of hardened and cynical seamen capable of hypnotizing and mobilizing some of the others, then the captain of the vessel can count on a rough passage. With a combination of booze, drugs, and the inevitable tensions of men enclosed in a confined space, the situation can come perilously close to a marine version of gang warfare.

This interpretation may or may not be true. It certainly has the rather suspicious sound of the scape-goat syndrome, on the part of authorities, but, on the other hand, I don't think I'd trust Sailor as far as I could spit. Seamen are sometimes turned off ships at Port Said and sent home, under whatever pretext. I would venture to guess that this is what has happened to Sailor.

The Wanderbirds, all except Cheryl, sit with Sailor in the pavilion one day, from eight in the morning until late at night, their voices growing more bitterly querulous. Next day I ask Cheryl what it was that Sailor got the others onto.

"Speed," she says. "Derek took fifteen. Then tranquillizers, so they wouldn't get so far out they couldn't come back."

In this part of the world, amphetamines can be bought with no trouble at all at your friendly Port Said chemist shop. I'm slightly astonished when the Wanderbirds finally surface, weary, burned-out, but alive. Whether they survive or not is still up to them. With the Sailor, though, it isn't quite that way.

"He's into everything, I guess," Cheryl says calmly, and I see I am the naive one, not her. "Know how he makes enough to keep his habit? He and his brother keep a whorehouse in Philadelphia—well, anyway, that's what he says. I wouldn't guess he'd be that organized."

Sardonically attractive, personable, well-mannered, ruthless, and a compulsive liar, Sailor could be described as a psychopath. But that's too simple. Something about that semi-ruined face reminds me of a line from a poem, a long-ago poem by Edwin Markham, a line which has stayed in my head for countless years, and now surfaces: "Whose breath blew out the light within this brain?"

Both Sailor and the Wanderbirds are temporary

exiles, but there is another group of exiles here, the strangest I have ever met, for they are expatriates in their own country.

"*Mon dieu*," Mr. Kamal says plaintively. "Can it be necessary to nationalize everything?"

He happens to be a merchant. Some of his friends are professional men and some work for the Canal Authority, carrying on the administrative jobs they held under the old Canal Company. The group, as a cultural phenomenon, was created by the canal. They are Egyptians, yet they are not Muslims but Roman Catholics, and French rather than Arabic is their first language. They lived for several generations in a society which had its feet in Egypt but its eyes on France. Mr. Kamal is slight, nervous, gently witty. His wife is extremely *chic* and would be completely at ease in Paris. She wears a black suit, perfectly tailored, a turquoise silk blouse, spidery heels, the right gloves. They speak only French between themselves, and when they speak Arabic, sometimes they falter. With me, they politely speak English, in which they are fluent.

"We are too Europeanized, my sweetness," he says.

And she, focusing away from the unbearable, spotlights her own known territory.

"I am your sweetness?" she says. "That is nice."

They meet friends nightly at Gianola's Café, "the only decent café left nowadays." Over coffee and pastries, they recall a lost era which for them was happier. Now their lives are full of disagreeable trivialities.

"I used to read *Marie-Claire* all the time," a maiden lady tells me, "but these days it is quite impossible to get the French magazines." Almonds and apricots are not imported any more. "Souvenir, souvenir," Mr. Kamal says of the nut-and-fruit-laden days of yore. One cannot help thinking of the *fellahin*, Egypt's peasant-farmers, whose memories of yesteryear almost certainly did not include almonds and apricots. Yet the sadness of these French-oriented Egyptians is real and Chekhovian. The world, incomprehensibly, has altered, and they are left here, mourning a dead past, unable to relate to any present-day, strangers in the only country they are permitted to call home.

Friends saunter in and out of Gianola's. The captain of a canal dredger tells Mrs. Kamal about her horoscope, which he has recently read.

"You will wrestle with temptation like a priest wrestling with Satan."

Mrs. Kamal listens, all interest.

"And will I win?" she asks demurely.

"Oh yes," he says confidently.

"What a pity," Mrs. Kamal says, with a twinkle of naughtiness, glancing at her husband. This is their game, to tease one another, and it communicates both need and affection. They must play games, for reality is too harsh and their dilemmas cannot be solved. They want, in some ways, to leave the country, but they cannot bring themselves to leave everything behind, not only their financial assets but their friends and their memories as well. When they speak of London or Paris, it is of the cities they knew some twenty years ago. They do not really know that Europe, too, has changed. I am reminded, more than anything, of the old hymn, "There is a happy land, far far away." It is their soul's refuge, this mythical and non-existent land, while they sip coffee at Gianola's, waiting for death to transport them out of history.

The near past is often painful, but the past beyond living memory has had its thorns trimmed and survives as dates and events rather than people. Occasionally, however, an individual presence breaks through, sometimes tragically, sometimes ludricrously—as with the letter the British consul discovered in the basement when the consulate (now tactfully designated as "Canadian Consulate—British Shipping Interests," although the Consul himself is a Brit, needless to say) was re-opened in Port Said a year ago. Dated 12th April 1845, the epistle was from a firm in Cairo and was addressed to one W. Manson. "Dear Sir—We beg to inform you that we have this day sent to your address a cage containing nine canaries, the balance of the twenty-four as originally advised as having been purchased by your order, and regret to say that fifteen of them have died, not withstanding our having taken every care of them, and now send up the dead ones along with the others . . ." Unfortunate and probably irate Mr. Manson, landed with all those dead canaries. Dates and facts and figures pale beside such letters as these, and even I, anti-imperialist from a long way back, can visualize and sympathize with individual twits.

In less than two years, the Suez Canal will embark on its second century of life. Once the canal epitomized a Victorian world of opulent trade and the self-righteous certainties of colonialism. Now it exists in a world seared with uncertainties, and in a Middle East feverish with rival Arab nationalisms. Its operation and maintenance epitomize a healthy aspect of

Egyptian pride, while its position appears to encourage a pharaonic and unhealthy desire to expand power and spheres of influence. Even though the supertankers have shown that it is not the only practicable route, the canal will probably continue to be international shipping's main entrance to the increasingly essential oil of the sheikhdoms. In 1969, the Suez Canal will be a hundred years old. Whatever the second century brings, it will never bring human indifference towards those 173 kilometers of liquid roadway through the desert.

This story of my various air adventures was published in 1974. Since then, I've been on a lot of planes. Thank goodness, my flights in recent years have been relatively uneventful ones. But the imagination grows not less but more bizarre with the passing of the years. On a recent flight, the cabin lights kept flicking on and off in strange sequences—two here, three there. Could it be, I wondered, that extraterrestrial creatures were attempting to communicate with this very plane? The flights I've loved most in the last few years have been those going west. Coming across Ontario into Manitoba, you soon know you are above the prairies, because you look down and see how vast the farms are, the great sweep of that land divided into sections and quarter sections, and the soil that true rich black, which, because I grew up there, always seems to me the only right colour for soil to be.

The Wild Blue Yonder

A sizable portion of my adult life has been spent up in the air. I mean that statement literally, as it happens, although I suppose that figuratively it might be true as well. I am, of course, referring to that well-known easy mode of transport, the airplane. What the airlines aim at, or so I imagine, is a journey both smooth and soothing, punctuated only by the heavy chomping of passengers' jaws as they work their way through the interminable grub which appears with monotonous regularity on all flights except those when you are really hungry, on which occasions something invariably goes wrong and the dinner is delayed until ten minutes before you land. The airlines have the quaint notion that this constant masticating of bits of stringy chicken or beef, plus the usual peas and potato croquettes, not to mention the unmentionable custard trifle desserts, will relieve the passengers' edginess and keep them safely out of mischief so that they won't bother one another or the stewardesses, who are certainly overworked because of all the meal serving and the unnecessary offering of liqueurs to people who (and that's most of us) never have them at home. This is known as circular reasoning, but it doesn't work. As a seasoned air traveller, I can honestly say that I have hardly ever known a flight to be uneventful.

I am not, of course, talking about such an event as being airsick, which is not only dull but which I have always believed to be all in the head and totally unnecessary, mainly because I myself happen to have a cast-iron stomach. No. I am talking about those little occurrences which prevent one from becoming bored during the long hours of soaring above the earth.

The first flight of my life (not counting the ten-minute ride I had for half a dollar in a miniature aircraft with one of the old-fashioned barnstormers when I was about ten) was from Aden to London in 1952, when my husband and I were returning from Somaliland after a two-year tour there. We had gone out to Africa by ship, so for me this was an exciting experience. What kept the trip even more sprightly was the lanky middle-aged lady sitting across the aisle from me. She twitched and jittered like a sad ostrich with a severe nervous affliction.

"Do you think it's safe?" she leaned over to ask me. "The plane, I mean. It doesn't *feel* safe."

This was, remember, more than twenty years ago,

in the days before air travel became as much taken for granted as hopping onto a bus. I assumed one of my more phony masks, that of perfect assurance.

"Certainly," I said. "Absolutely safe. Nothing to it."

"It's my first flight," she twittered, "and I'm just terrified. What if anyone gets sick? I mean, really *ill*. Like a heart attack."

This was ever such a cheery thought to me. I was not in any imminent danger of having a heart attack, but I happened to be eight months pregnant, and I so much resembled a galleon in full sail that it wouldn't have surprised me if my child had begun to arrive any moment.

"Not to worry," I said with stunning dishonesty. "All the stewardesses are trained nurses."

"Really? Are you sure?"

"Positive," I said. "It's the law."

Naturally, I had no idea whether they were trained nurses or not, although it seemed unlikely that they would be. Anything, however, to shut up my friend across the aisle.

On my next flight, we were headed back to Africa, this time to Ghana, with our three-month-old daughter. On the plane was another young couple, Irish, with their baby of about the same age. Their baby howled non-stop for hour upon hour upon hour. Our marvellous kid scarcely murmured for most of the time, but alas, in the final lap of the journey, the other child dropped into an exhausted sleep and our daughter raised her very considerable voice. The Irishman came over and beamed affectionately at me.

"I hope you won't take offence," he said, "but the foinest moment in me life was when *your* baby began to cry!"

One of my most unforgettable experiences in flight was Marilyn. We were returning to Ghana after a leave in England, accompanied by our daughter, aged three, and our son, aged six months. At the airport in London, while we were waiting for the flight to be called, a girl wandered up to us. And what a girl. She had long blonde hair and looked very much like Marilyn Monroe, which is why I've always thought of her by that name. Slender, beautifully dressed, sophisticated. She made me feel like a slob, with my left shoulder permanently damp from my small son's upburped milk. Then she opened her mouth and spoke.

"Par'n me," she said in an unbelievably little-girl voice, "is the Port of Disembarkation where you get *on* or where you get *off*?"

She had a form to fill out, and was totally flummoxed. We informed her of the meaning of disembarkation, and she was so grateful she never left our sides for the entire trip.

"How old do you think I am?" she asked me.

"I dunno. Twenty?"

"Uh-uh," Marilyn said pathetically. "That's my trouble. People always take me for older and so they think I'll know what to do, but I don't. I'm sixteen, actually. I come from Sacramento and I've never been away from my home not even for one night in my whole life until now. I got married a few months ago to this Air Force fella, see, but we spent our honeymoon at my home. I was Miss Sacramento last year, and everybody thought I was *much older*."

Stacked like that, who wouldn't?

She was going to a U.S. Air Force base in North Africa to join her husband. Her flight had been delayed, and now she was frantically worried lest her husband would not be there to meet her. Had she cabled him from London, we asked. Well, gee, no, she actually hadn't thought of that. We were in mid-air at the time, so it was a bit late. I have never in my entire life met anyone as naive as Marilyn. Many nine-year-olds would be knowledgeable by comparison.

Sure enough, when we reached the airport in North Africa, Marilyn's husband was nowhere to be seen. For us, it was a very short stop—we had about ten minutes before the flight took off again, and no time to lose. My husband rushed off to phone the u.s. Air Force base, while I attempted to mop up Marilyn's flooding tears. At that precise moment, our small daughter threw up all over the airport floor, and our even smaller son in the sodden depths of his Karri-Kot began yelling his lungs out. It was one of those moments when you ask yourself why you ever left home.

Our flight was called. We plonked Marilyn down firmly in a waiting room chair. We had visions of her being spirited away and disappearing forever into the harem of some Tuareg chieftain.

"Now don't move," we told her sternly, "until you see either your husband or some accredited representative of the American Air Force. Understand? Don't *budge!*"

In the intervening years, Marilyn's beautiful clueless face has sometimes crossed my mind, and I wonder if her husband ever did turn up, or if she is still sitting there in Idris Airport, Libya, waiting.

Flights to and from Africa in those pre-jet days were lengthy—about twenty hours, as I recall. And sometimes they were fraught with small excitements, such as the time I woke up in the dawn, looked out the window on one side, craned my neck to get a glimpse out of the window on the other side, and perceived that exactly half our engines, one on either side, were no longer operative. Shaking, I called the stewardess.

"Oh, don't worry, dear," she said calmly. "They've been like that all night."

Those were thrilling times, all right. In later years, the flights, now jet, became swifter although possibly not that much safer than they had previously been. I have always had a very philosophical outlook on the subject. If the plane crashes, one will at least depart this vale of tears quickly, or so I must believe. I have never worried much about it whilst in the air. On one occasion, however, when I was flying back to Canada from Africa, by myself with the children, my cool nearly disappeared. I couldn't sleep and had finished the book I'd brought, so the stewardess kindly gave me a magazine to read. I turned to the lead article. The title was as follows: "Great Air Disasters of the Past Decade." When the stewardess next passed by, I mildly suggested to her that this was one magazine she might consider withdrawing from circulation.

Air travelling with young children can be great fun, provided you have a fairly dark and even sick sense of humour. Like the time at Lagos airport when my eighteen-month-old son rushed gleefully up to a table in the restaurant, gave the cloth a decisive tug, and brought down several stacks of plates in shattered fragments. Or the time on the same awful flight when he accidentally poked a breadstick into his sister's eye, leaving her in highly vocal agony for the next four hours or so. The trick about travelling with little kids is to take along enough books, puzzles, games, crayons, plasticine, etcetera, to keep them amused until the first meal is served. After that, all you need to do is keep the sick bag at the ready and keep telling them, "Yes, love, we'll soon be there." On no account ever raise your voice to them, or even hiss dire threats under your breath. If you do, they will, understandably enough, howl blue murder. And you will not like the looks you receive from other passengers.

A woman travelling alone by plane can sometimes find herself in slightly strange situations. Like, would you believe an occasion when a travelling salesman tries to seduce you in mid-flight? It happened to me once on my lone way from London to Karachi. The blankets were handed out by the stewardess, and the lights turned off for the night. There were three seats in the row, but only two were occupied. Me and the salesman. He began by expressing the opinion that we'd both be much more comfortable if we removed the arm-rests between the seats. I, however, thought otherwise. After a weary night spent in fending off this clown, my inborn sense of tact and politeness was wearing decidedly thin.

"Well, at least it must be a change from the farmer's daughter," I sourly commented.

He was an Englishman. I don't think he even got the wisecrack.

Some of my most memorable flights have been those taken with my kids when they became older, old enough to pack and carry their own suitcases and to do some background reading on the places we were seeing. I was once commissioned by a magazine to do several articles on Egypt. My son was at that time eleven, and my daughter was fourteen. We had a glorious month in Egypt, and I enjoyed the whole thing far more than I would have done if they had not been with me. But the trip was not without its plane adventures. We were due to fly from Cairo to Luxor, and all the way from the hotel to the airport, I kept telling the local representatives of Cook's Travel Agency that we were going to miss the plane. The bus had, naturally, been half an hour late. But in that Islamic country all is in the hands of Allah. If you are destined to catch the plane, you'll catch it. If not, forget it and stop worrying. We arrived at Cairo airport with about four seconds to spare. There remains engraved on my memory the picture of myself and my kids pelting across the tarmac as though in training for the Olympics, followed by three Cook's men with our suitcases on their heads. We puffed up to the plane just in time to join the queue of ascending passengers. The stewardess then appeared in the doorway.

"This flight," she announced, "has been delayed one hour."

The Cook's representatives glared at me reproachfully. See—Allah knew what He was doing.

My *pièce de résistance*, however, in terms of air travel, was the time I was locked in the lavatory on a plane going from Aden to Hargeisa. It happened thus. In 1966, the Somali Republic had broken off diplomatic relations with Britain, owing to the two countries' differing views on the Somalis in the northern province of Kenya. Despite this break, however, the government of the republic invited some ten people from England to go out, expenses paid, to take part in the Independence Day celebrations. These included people who had once worked in education or administration or radio or linguistics in that country, all old friends or acquaintances of mine. And because of a small book of Somali poetry and prose translations I had done years ago, with much help and assistance from others, it included me.

We flew from London to Aden, where we stayed overnight. We then proceeded to Somaliland by a dinky aircraft which, if not actually held together with chewing gum, gave the impression of belonging to an era before ours. All went well, however, until I stepped into the lavatory. The bolt on the door didn't seem to fit too well, and I had to struggle to get it locked. When I tried to unlock it, it wouldn't. Again and again I attacked the stubborn metal, but it refused to yield.

Help! I had visions of the plane landing at Hargeisa, the old Somali friends there to welcome us, and me locked in the john. Having to be rescued with a blowtorch. Humiliation. Disaster. What to do? I yelled pleadingly to the steward. He was very sympathetic, but of course didn't know what to do. Neither did any of my co-travellers, who by this time were gathered in an interested little group outside the lavatory door. Finally, with one of those incredible bursts of strength which desperation can sometimes create, and at great cost to the skin of my hands, I got the bolt to give way. Trembling, I staggered forth to the accompaniment of rousing cheers on all sides. Rarely have I experienced such a dramatic moment. I later discovered from another passenger who had also visited the john that if I'd been stuck there for some hours I wouldn't have starved. It was a very small plane, and the sandwiches for lunch were stashed away, in practical manner, in a tiny cabinet above the toilet.

One experience I've never had on a plane is that of being hijacked. You wonder how long your luck can last. I'm checking the boat and train schedules.

I was based at Elm Cottage, in Buckinghamshire, England, for ten years. It was there that I wrote many of my books, including most of the "Manawaka" books. I came back to Canada frequently during those years on visits and subsequently to work on my novel *The Diviners* at my cottage on the Otonabee River during the summers of 1971, 1972, and 1973. I have always had a very strong sense of place, and Elm Cottage remains in my mind as a place of important memories, the place where I did much of my work and where my children grew up. This article is relatively frivolous, perhaps because any deeper feelings about our life in Elm Cottage (nicknamed Elmcot) seemed and still seem to be a private matter. The dedication in *The Diviners*, however, reads: "For the Elmcot people, past present and future, and for the house itself, with love and gratitude."

✿

Put Out One or Two More Flags

Sometimes I'm asked by North Americans what it is like to live in a quiet quaint English village. I have to reply in all honesty that I don't know. This village is not as steadfastly quiet as you might suppose. It is on the main Oxford road and the cars tend to swoosh through as though no village were here at all, causing local residents to raise their walking sticks or umbrellas and utter loud but futile imprecations. As for quaintness—well, I don't think the village would qualify there, either. True, our shopping centre contains the following *only*: a butcher's, a grocer's, a post-office which lives in a small candy shop, a pub, an antique shop in which I have never seen any customers, and a secondhand bookshop which very oddly also sells plastic flower arrangements. True, there is the occasional cheerily eccentric vicar and a stentorian-voiced tweedy lady or so. True, there are some lovely old flint-and-brick houses and a village pond which (according to local legend) in bygone days was used as a witches' ducking pond, where crones were held under water for minutes at a time in order to determine scientifically whether or not they were guilty of the dark arts. And when I first moved here, there used to be a delicate old lady who wore a black lace mantilla and chuffed through the village in a small electric car of truly ancient vintage, while her delicate old dog scuffled along beside her. All the same, it couldn't really be said to be your actual quainte olde English village full of Tudor half-timbering circa 1930.

These, however, are not the main reasons why I don't feel terribly knowledgeable about village life. I am involved elsewhere. Rupert Brooke, you will recall, wrote about "some corner of a foreign field that is for ever England." His lines were written in a somewhat gloomier context, but although I am not buried here yet, I take his meaning to heart. I live on two-thirds of an English acre which appears to be the maple leaf forever. To put it bluntly, the place is crawling with Canadians. And, supporter of integration though I always have been, I have to admit I like it this way. I didn't plan it. It simply happened.

When I moved here, I wondered what life would be like in a peaceful quaint English village. Would I be totally isolated, surrounded only by beautiful trees, unspeaking and unspeakably snobbish squires, or villagers whose conversational ploys would consist of "Arrgh! 'Tis a broight day, innit, missus?" Some of the county gents and their ladies are here, all right,

and some of them speak to me and some of them
don't. The villagers are the true population, some
families having lived here for hundreds of years as
gardeners, artisans, shopkeepers, tenant farmers. They
speak in a soft and beautiful Buckinghamshire accent,
and are friendly and accepting towards strangers such
as myself. Still, you would never become a villager
until you'd lived here half a century, and probably
not then. When I discovered these general patterns, I
thought that life here might be rather lonely. Then
the Canadian contingents began to arrive. At first it
was mainly my contemporaries, and I realized with
surprise and delight that if I stayed here long enough,
every person I knew in Canada would ultimately turn
up. I believe it was Henry James who used to refer
to summer as The Great North American Visiting
Season. Now it's the whole year. And it's not only
my contemporaries any more. These days, our visitors
are just as likely to be the sons and daughters of old
friends, or my nieces and nephews, or a wide assortment of young Canadian writers.

"This damn place is like a combination of London
Airport, a third-class hotel, and a recording studio," I
sometimes pathetically moan, on one of those days
when the air seems just that little bit too full of guitar
sounds, and we've run out of clean sheets and towels,
and I can't think what to have for dinner. "It's chaos,
that's what it is. I swear I'm going to take the vow
in a silent Order."

Then, unexpectedly, somebody says they reckon it's
their turn to make dinner, and no thanks, they won't
put the groceries on the bill—they'll go and buy what
they need for the speciality they have in mind. And
somebody else offers to do the laundry this week. And

after dinner we listen to the song somebody has just composed. And I have the sense of an extended family group, a good feeling. My son and daughter, who have lived in this country for nine years, feel deep connections here because this house is their home, but they also feel Canadian, which is small wonder considering the accents around the place.

Our house is called Elm Cottage and was, we believe, so-named more than a hundred years ago after the giant elm in the garden. It is not the North American idea of a cottage, as it has six bedrooms. The oldest part of the house is some two hundred years old, the rest being about ninety. It was not, as some have suggested, designed by a lunatic. It must simply have grown, bits being added hither and thither. Now we have nameplates on the doors, having had numerous visitors who got lost on the way to the bathroom or who were totally unable to find the kitchen. When I ordered the nameplates in a nearby town, I told the girl in the shop what I wanted. Each name had its good reasons. *Steproom*, one of the bedrooms, was because you have to go down a step when entering it and if you forget this essential fact you will fall flat on your face. *Dwarf Room* used to be the dressing-room for the master bedroom, and when we turned it into an extra bedroom a friend commented that it would be a dandy place for visiting dwarfs.

"Coo," the shop girl said, impressed. "Novelty names!"

I felt like Walt Disney and nearly cancelled the order.

As in most old houses in England, the deadly fight against dry rot and rising damp is never really over, but we're slightly ahead at the moment, or so we fondly believe until the next wet patch appears on a ceiling or wall. Among the many charms of the place is the sign on the tank over the toilet, which says PONTIFEX'S NO-SOUND. This Victorian appellation cannot be said to be entirely accurate. Every time you flush the thing it sounds like a fourteen-cannon salute. The house is heated with gas, coal, wood, and electricity, in various corners, which to some Canadians seems enough quaintness to be getting on with. No central heating, needless to say. Once ten fireplaces were used here; now only two of them are in use. The heat loss must be staggering, despite our valiant attempts to block off the unused chimneys. In winter it is advisable to wear three sweaters at all times.

Nonetheless, we do have mutedly shining red stone tile floors, and a lot of smallish rooms so people can either congregate or be by themselves, and two interestingly neurotic cats, and a rose garden which keeps on blooming until nearly Christmas. There is a kind of shabby elegance about the place which I've always loved. Nearly all our Canadian visitors seem to feel the same. If someone says (as once happened with a CBC-TV interviewer who shall remain nameless), "Margaret, I just don't see how you can possibly live in a place like this," then they don't get asked back.

Our Canadian stronghold has obviously made its mark on the village. Once, Al Purdy and his wife Eurithe stayed with us for several weeks on their way back to Canada from Greece. This was the origin of the saying in our house when offering someone a tin of beer, "Do you want a small tin or an Al-sized one?" Al immediately discovered that the village bookshop contained a whole lot of old Canadian books, which were of no apparent interest to anyone in England but of considerable interest and value back home. He bought dozens, packaging them up and posting them to Canada. Some time later, when I was in the village post-office, Miss Wright behind the wicket sighed nostalgically.

"Not the same as it was when Mr. Purdy was here, is it?" she said.

The local P.O. probably hadn't done so well out of stamp sales in two hundred years.

The village has taken note of us in other ways as well. Not long ago, one of the young writers whom I'd met in Toronto came to spend a week with us. He and his girl were hitching, and when they arrived in the village they stopped at a local garage and asked the way to the street on which we live. The garage man needed only to hear their Canadian accents.

"Oh, you'll be looking for Mrs. Laurence's house," he said. "First street on your left and about halfway up the hill."

One of my nieces recently came to stay with us for a while. Apparently she had told a friend back home she was coming. The friend was taking a Canadian Literature course on which one of my novels was being taught.

"Doesn't she live in a castle or something in England?" the girl enquired.

"Yeh," my niece replied ironically. "Elm Castle."

I liked this concept very much. Just about this time I had lost my longtime cleaning lady to the canteen of the local primary school.

"When I clean this dump," I told my niece, "it begins to feel castle-size."

Since then, however, the advantages of many Canadian visitors have once more become manifest. When the house needs cleaning, everyone who happens to be here at the moment takes on a couple of rooms. Somebody always offers to do the dishes or make after-dinner coffee. One young Canadian calls this system "agreeable anarchy," which means that we all fulfil what we conceive to be our individual responsibilities, and astonishingly enough, it all seems to mesh.

I wrote to a friend in Toronto not long ago, telling her the old hostel was back in business after my absence in Canada last summer. I also mentioned that our status was now that of Castle. Concerned about the novel which I am attempting to write, she wrote back as follows: "Your North American Home Service is quick to offer their assistance. Our eminent architect, Everard Turnpenny Cetera, has drawn you an individualized castle plan which he feels is exactly suited to your needs. We await only your signature to begin the demolition of your present and obviously outmoded residence and the construction of a more economic and generally satisfying dwelling."

Enclosed was a drawing of the New Elm Castle, complete with rope ladder ("For ingress to the castle, Sundays only") and a moat containing barracuda. Also enclosed was a design for a dual-purpose castle banner. Hoisted one way it reads "*Moi Libre:* Me Free." Hoisted the other, it is a frantic appeal which reads "*Libre Moi:* Free Me." This is in case the visiting contingents ever reach proportions which make writing impossible for me, owing to a plethora of potato-peeling, pie-making and the like.

Some of the Canadians who have come to visit have remained in England, at least for the time being. The young couple who came over to hold the fortress the year I was writer-in-residence at the University of

Toronto are now living in a village only a few miles away, working, writing, composing songs. A small but enthusiastic colony, mostly writers or composers, appears to be growing in Buckinghamshire. It has been suggested that this whole process is in fact a plot—if not actually to take over England, at least to mount a propaganda campaign. I neither affirm nor deny. All I can say is that over the years I have observed that only when a British diplomat is kidnapped or when our Prime Minister either slides down a banister or gets married is there ever any Canadian news reported in the British press. I have also observed that although many African books are published here and, what is more, reviewed, very little of the interesting Canadian writing which has been done in the past decade has found a publisher here. It may yet be that Elm Castle will be the headquarters for an infiltration movement. Despite my Presbyterian background, there has always been a faint streak of the wild-eyed evangelist in me.

Move over, High Commissioner, sir. The Low Commissioner is operating from Unofficial Canada House.

Published in 1966, this article now seems to me to be an early working-out, in non-fiction, of a theme I would later, in *The Diviners*, express in fiction, namely the feelings a person has when making the pilgrimage to the land of the ancestors. My ancestors, as I make clear in the article, were not Highland Scots; they came from Fifeshire, in the Lowlands. But I always felt my spiritual ancestors were Highlanders, and possibly that is why I gave Morag Gunn, in *The Diviners*, ancestors who came from Sutherland and who were turned out during the Highland Clearances. But this, my first view of Scotland, was in some strange way also my first true understanding of where I belonged, namely the land where I was born. It seems odd to me now that, at the time I wrote this article, I had already written *The Stone Angel*, set mainly in Manawaka, a fictional prairie town, and had also written *A Jest of God*, published the same year as this article, set also in Manawaka. It is as though in my fiction I knew exactly where to go, but in my life I didn't, as yet. It also seems interesting that I came to a greater understanding of the Scots' clan system through a certain amount of knowledge of the tribal system in Africa. Incidentally, when this article was published, someone wrote to inform me that William Shakespeare really hadn't been a Scot.

Road from the Isles

I was brought up on Scottish music. I could sing "Just a wee doch an' doris, just a wee drap that's a'" at a quite touchingly young age, although it is true that at the time I believed Doc and Doris to be the names of two people. I learned such songs as "I Belong to Glasgee" and "Road to the Isles" from my grandmother on my father's side. We made no finicky dis-

158

tinctions between what was genuine and what was music-hall. The songs of Harry Lauder, to my mind, went as far back in history and were as much traditional Scottish music as "The Pibroch of Donal Dhu." My grandmother Wemyss was born in Ontario, and her knowledge of Scotland was probably about the same as her knowledge of Timbuktu. My grandfather Wemyss was born in Scotland, but he died shortly after I was born, so I never had the opportunity of gleaning any information from him.

Nevertheless, as a child I was extremely aware of my Scottish background. No one could ever tell me whether my family had been Lowlanders or Highlanders, because no one in the prairie town where I grew up seemed very certain exactly where that important dividing line came on the map of Scotland. I decided, therefore, that my people had come from the Highlands. In fact, they had not, but Highlanders seemed more interesting and more noble to me in every way. My concept of what Highlanders were like was based upon Alan Breck in *Kidnapped*.

My family had belonged to a branch of the clan MacDuff, and when I first read *Macbeth*—written by that famous Scot, William Shakespeare—I felt myself to be the near kin of the Thane of Fife. We possessed certain trophies from the past, which I used to handle with curiosity and reverence, as though they had been religious relics. One of these was a silver plaid pin which bore our family crest. This crest was a bird that remained mysteriously unidentified. My father believed it to be a cormorant and my mother believed it to be an undersized emu. Our family motto, I regret to say, was *Je Pense*—"I Think"—which seemed to me both tame and boastful. I would have preferred

the gruesomely ferocious war cry of the Camerons
—"Sons of the hound, come here and get flesh!"

I do not remember at what age the disenchantment
set in, but gradually I began to perceive that I was
no more Scots than I was Siamese. Whatever of the
Old Country had filtered down to me could roughly
be described as Mock Scots. The Scotland I had en-
visaged as a child had been a fantasy, appealing because
it seemed so much more bold and high-hearted than
the prairie town where I really lived.

When at last, not so very long ago, I planned to visit
the Highlands of Scotland, I did not know what to
expect of the reality. I felt absolutely no connection
with the actual Scotland, and yet I half expected and
even hoped to discover some feeling of ancestry there,
something that would convey to me a special personal
meaning. My ignorance of Scottish history was total.
The only thing the last Jacobite rebellion meant to
me was the label on the Drambuie bottle, "A Link
With The '45." All I knew of the Clearances was that
they had had something to do with sheep. I knew a
good deal about the Selkirk settlers, but only after
they reached Canada.

I began to read. Such books as John Prebble's *The
Highland Clearances* and Ian Grimble's *The Trial of
Patrick Sellars* made the story come alive—the breakup
of the Highland clans which culminated at the Battle
of Culloden, and the subsequent betrayal of the Highlanders by their own chiefs, as the glens were cleared
of unprofitable people to make room for profitable
sheep. This must surely be one of the most painful
episodes in European history, the tale of how the
Gaelic-speaking people of northern Scotland were

driven from the lands they had worked for centuries, treated as sub-human by the English-speaking bailiffs who burned their dwellings, and ignored by land-owners who preferred the lights of Edinburgh or London. Some of the evicted crofters lived thinly from what food they could trawl from the rocky wind-sullen coast. Others, in a kind of numb bewilder-ment, were herded aboard the emigrant ships and found themselves facing the desperate heat of Aus-tralia or the treacherous winters of Canada.

The Highland clan system was similar to tribal sys-tems anywhere. The chief was believed in, not so much as an individual as a symbol, a father, a king figure who possessed almost mystical powers of pro-tection and strength. To be betrayed by one of these must have been like knowing, really knowing, that one's own father intended, if he could, to murder you. The outcast Highlanders must have arrived in Canada as a people bereft, a people who had been wounded psychically in ways they could not possibly have com-prehended. Throughout the Clearances, they were never able to produce strong leaders from among their ranks, for the concept of the chief as the trusted and only leader was too firmly entrenched. Their few uprisings were for the most part unorganized and pathetically inadequate. Many of them left their land with no protest at all, with the voiceless docility of the sheep which replaced them. They had been fighters —the Highland regiments were famous for their fight-ing men—but during the hundred years of the Clear-ances, they fought scarcely at all, not even with words. They only mourned. They had been in the deepest possible ways forsaken; in the truest sense their hearts had been broken. This, not the romantic swashbuckling figures in Sir Walter Scott's novels, was the reality of the Highlanders.

I had known, of course, as every person schooled in Canada knows, of the external difficulties of the early Scottish settlers, the people of Glengarry and Red River. What I had never seen before was a glimpse of their inner terrors, a sense of the bereavement they must have carried with them like a weight of lead in the soul. What appeared to be their greatest trouble in a new land—the grappling with an unyielding environment—was in fact probably their salvation. I believe they survived not in spite of the physical hardships but *because* of them, for all their attention and thought *had* to be focused outward. They could not brood. If they had been able to do so, it might have killed them.

When I left for Inverness, I felt strangely divided in mind between what I had been reading and the imaginary Scotland of my childhood. The story of the Highland Clearances, which I had been learning for the first time, moved me very much. It could scarcely fail to move anyone. But I still could not see what personal meaning all this could have for me, although I felt it must have some. I hoped I would find out.

Euston Station was crowded and dirty as usual, the waiting room awash with spilled tea and the ashes of ten million cigarettes. Beside my kids and I sat a man and a woman, also waiting for the Royal Highlander, the night train to Inverness. I don't know what wedding or funeral or football match they had come south for, but they must have been celebrating, or holding the wake, as the case may be, for several days. They were in pretty poor shape. The man fell asleep, but the woman sang. "I never felt more like singing the blues," she croaked hoarsely, and I believed her. She was in alien territory. She felt it, and resented it, and resented feeling it.

"Where do you think they took me?" she said. "To Hampstead—to the courts they took me, and they fined me two quid. Two bloody quid they fined me, my dear."

Her voice was angry and sad, melodious in a way her singing had not been, and this was the first time I had heard the accent of the Highlands.

"But I am just as good as they are," she said, "and I'll tell you one thing, my dear—the people here has no consideration, none whatsoever."

She turned to her companion and began blowing softly into his ear.

"Whist! Come, man—come along, Milton, wake up now."

What a name for a Scot, I thought. Milton, thou shouldst be waking at this hour; Scotland hath need of thee. But Milton, and perhaps the Highlands with him, slept on.

The journey from London to Inverness takes all night. A jolting indecisive half-sleep is always my portion on trains, and when I decided to give up and to get up that dawn, it was with a feeling of interior gauntness that made the entire countryside seem even more stark than it was. The hills were steep and rocky. The grass was sparse, but the land was forested with fir and pine and slender birch with moss around the roots. The water of the burns was brown and clear. In the grey light of the morning, something about the land looked familiar to me, but the reason eluded me.

We moved away from the hills and onto a moor. Then a station, and the name—*Culloden.* There is always some sense of astonishment, for me, at actually being in a place where a great event once happened. The event at Culloden was a tragic one, for it was here that the clans were broken at last and the hereditary jurisdiction of the chiefs finally destroyed. The Highland people never rose again against the redcoats and the southern throne. It was early spring, and so the heather was brown, a reddish brown, the colour of dried blood. The air was still, and the only sound was the clank and screech of the train as we stopped. The low hills around Culloden looked as though they had never been disturbed, not ever. The war cries and the pibrochs had faded a long time ago; nothing of that distant intensity seemed to cling around the moor now. But there is a legend that the heather will not grow over the earth where a clansman fell. I looked at the green swaths crescenting the ground, and wondered, and then the train moved on.

My children and I were going to stay with a friend who lives in a village on Cromarty Firth in the part of Ross-shire known as the Black Isle. As we drove out from Inverness, the cab driver obligingly pointed out the sights. An old church where one of the clans once very meanly attacked another who were unarmed while they worshipped. Then a new distillery. Then another old church. That was the Highlands for you, he said—all churches and distilleries.

At Beauly the grey-pink sandstone houses stand neatly and decorously as if daring anyone to find even a partial scandal in their past. No word, they seem to say, has ever been raised against the Establishment here; we are respectable folk in these parts.

"Yon monument," the cab driver said with a certain wryness, "was put up in memory of a local laird who raised a battalion from here for the Boer War."

But I did not see any monument in the streets of Beauly for the men of Ross who made a futile and courageous attempt to drive the sheep from the land in the riots of 1792, the year known to Highlanders as The Year of the Sheep. The earliest Clearances began around here, for it was here that the fat Cheviot, known as The Great Sheep, were first pastured in the Highlands. Some of the crofters of Ross—men of Beauly and Dingwall and the hills—drove six thousand of the lairds' sheep along Cromarty Firth, hoping to send them over into Inverness. It was not so much a riot as an isolated gesture of protest. The gentlemen of Ross, however, became extremely alarmed. The army was summoned to Dingwall, a village along the firth, and the crofters were captured and imprisoned. Their sentences varied—some were fined; one was to be sent to Botany Bay. But none of the sentences was carried out, because one night in the Dingwall prison the door was mysteriously opened and the ringleaders escaped, never to be heard of again.

Along Cromarty Firth, in these days, the wild swans gather. Each morning and evening we walked along the beach and watched them. They stay here summer and winter, making their nests in spring, hatching their cygnets, caring for them beyond the span of most birds, for it is well over a year before the ugly ducklings at last flaunt the white plumage of their kind. Just before dusk, the flotilla of swans would move out, along the firth, the tide coming in now over the mud flats where the spiralled shells and the crimson and jade-coloured stones lay dazzling with sea-wetness and where the yellow-brown kelp spread like scrum at the ebb tide. The dogs lolloped and the children plodded, looking mud-bound to the eyes of adults but in their own eyes hovering always on the possibility of buried treasure. The children had been warned about the nesting season, so they stayed well away from the guardian cob swans, the great males with their white wings unfurled furiously like schooners' sails. The female swans stayed at the nest, poised delicately above their shell-bound young. The dogs, spaniel and collie, splashed in the returning sea, and the children came back triumphant with intricately coiled shells and bits of blue glass filed into jewels by the abrasive sands.

In the mid-1800's, hereabouts, the ships kept leaving for the south, full of barley and oats, grain grown on the landlords' soil. The crofters were enduring famine at that time because the potato blight had turned their only available food into black rot. In 1847 the people of the Black Isle tried to halt the movement of a grain ship. They attacked it in Cromarty Firth and were about to drag it from the sea when the soldiers arrived and stopped them. At Invergordon, just across the firth, the army stood guard at the docks while the ships were loaded. The people of the hills and town threw stones and shouted "Starvation!" But the grain ships kept going south.

I sat on the shore as the evening gathered and watched the lights of Invergordon coming on, across the water, the low quiet lights of a quiet town. The wild swans sculled along the navy-blue water as though nothing except birds had ever happened here.

At Cromarty harbour one day we saw an amazing sight—a white-sailed schooner, fully rigged, gliding into the firth as though it were gliding in from a hundred years away. I thought of the British ships that had come here during the Crimean War to raise recruits for the Highland regiments. The Highlanders had gone to faraway wars for generations. Out of their warriors' tradition they had supplied many battalions for the alien crown. But by the mid-nineteenth century, they had had enough. Many of the glens that had once raised regiments were empty except for sheep. The men who remained were finished with foreign wars. Let the powers-that-be recruit the four-footed clansmen, they said bitterly—let them recruit sheep. When the British ships sailed into Cromarty harbour, the young men of Ross took to the hills.

I looked at the sailing ship, with its grace and balance and lightness, like a swan's, and wondered if it were a ghost-ship, a ghoul of a ship, forever hunting the men who had at last said *No*. The reality, I need hardly say, was otherwise. The ship we saw was the *Prince Louis*, owned and maintained by the school of Gordonstoun, where the contemporary bonnie Prince Charlie was then a pupil. They keep this vessel so that the boys can learn how to cope with a sailing ship, an accomplishment that must be mighty useful in the space age. And yet I question my own dubiety. My ten-year-old son watched the vessel for a long time, with enormous admiration, and then he said, "It's smashing!" Perhaps it is worthwhile, after all, that anachronistic ship, not for what it teaches, but for the chance, not often found today, to dream openly.

At Cromarty harbour, the old men sit, gossiping around the few fish-boats, around the few pleasure yachts owned by the few men of means. Almost all the people I saw in the streets of Cromarty were old, or at least—not to put too fine a point upon it—getting older. The young have mostly gone away, away to the south, to earn their living.

I walked with my children along the firth road one day, by the sea and over to an old church that has been abandoned for a century. It is a peculiar churchyard. It lies close by Invergordon, close by Dingwall, close to all that once happened here, and yet it is very much apart. Once it was a Roman Catholic church, where the priest dwelt and dispensed the Mass. The church itself is broken now, but the burial ground has been kept on. The oldest gravestones are overgrown with green-black moss; one cannot read the inscriptions. But the graves that bothered me were the ones from the mid-1800's. Perched on the tombstones, or nestling at their feet, were curious objects that looked like glass cake dishes, and inside these transparent cages were white flowers and doves and burgeoning leaves, still so starch-white that at first I took them to be plastic, the evidence of some inexplicable contemporary lunacy. But no, they were china, and had rested here these hundred years. Some of the glass cases were also covered with wire netting, an additional protection against the weather. Not against vandals—nothing like that, nothing so iconoclastic was a worry here, I was later told. I walked among these icing-sugar memorials and found myself wishing that the young men of Ross today would take the white china doves and dash them into the sea. But they are more sensible and, in truth, kinder. They do not desecrate the dead hands that have held them. They only leave, and go away to earn their living somewhere else.

The tourist trade is one industry that can bring employment and cash to the Highlands, and both are desperately needed. But strangers are spoken kindly to, it seemed to me, not only because of their cash but also because there is some deep courtesy in the people hereabouts. And yet there is a certain dichotomy. Some of the conversations I held—I as an outsider, inevitably gauche, feeling my way—seemed to indicate that there was a kind of bitter sadness about the whole tourist business. In the Black Isle some people referred to it sardonically as "the tartan dolly trade," the annual summer influx of people who want to see the Highlands as they never were nor evermore shall be.

The novelist Eric Linklater, a fighter by nature and a man who lives just across Cromarty Firth on the far side from where we were staying, has written a typically spirited introduction to Ian Grimble's book, *The Trial of Patrick Sellars*. Linklater speaks with humorous aggressiveness of the ranks of little Lowland girls, prancing and capering in a travesty of Highland male attire as they dance the Highland Fling at various acceptable Highland Games. I have the feeling that the Highlander of today is in somewhat the same position as the North American Indian. What he really was, in the past, is not comprehended by anyone outside his own tribe, but he has been taken up and glamourized and is expected to act a part. The Dance of the Ancestors—slicked-up, prettified, and performed forever in the same way. Nothing must ever change. The tourist trade wants everything to be settled and nice. Nothing must ever make reference to reality, to real sores, to *now*. The tourists are paying to be provided with an embodiment of their own fantasies. The local populace must surely sometimes want to say, "Look, it's not that way, not at all."

The hydro-development schemes are providing some employment in the Highlands, but the drift is still going on—the drift to the south, the removal of the young. When we left the village on Cromarty Firth, and drove back to Inverness, the young cab driver told me he was a mechanic and he asked me, "Would Canada be a good place to emigrate to?" I did not know how to reply. All I could say was, "Yes, I think it would probably be a good place to emigrate to, if you have a skill which is in demand there." Canada has been a good place, taken all around, for Scots to emigrate to, these hundred and fifty years. I wanted to tell him what the price would be, but I could not. I could not speak to him about the loneliness, or that his children would be the children of another land, not his, and that this difference would divide him from them forever. It is the fate of immigrants to discover this for themselves.

No places and no people reveal themselves quickly to the casual eye, and I knew this very well. Nevertheless, for the first time Scotland had become real to me, both in its past and in its present. For myself, however, I still did not feel any personal sense of connection with its history. The story of the Highland Clearances moved me as much as the story of the slave trade in Africa, but no more. For me, the ghosts were of another kind. It was the names I could not get away from. At the further end of Loch Ness, the home of the mythical monster, not so far away from where we were visiting, was Glengarry, where the eviction of the crofters continued for a century, and when they were over, twenty thousand Macdonells were in Canada and nearly none in Scotland. Not far away, also, in the opposite direction, was

Kildonan in Sutherland, where so many of the Mathesons, Macbeths, Bannermans, Gunns, and Mackays were evicted and cast their uncertain lot with the Earl of Selkirk, who made them part of his compulsion and his dream, the founding of a settlement at the junction of the Red and Assiniboine rivers, in a land he knew very little about. All these names meant something to me. Glengarry—this is Glengarry, Ontario; it is *The Man from Glengarry* by Ralph Connor. Sutherland, Bannerman, Ross, Selkirk, Kildonan—to me, these are the names of the places I grew up among, the names of Manitoba towns and the names of Winnipeg's streets. Weirdly, encountering them in Scotland, they seemed unreal there, or else derived, because to me they are Canadian names.

I realized why my first sight of the Highlands had seemed familiar, the spruce and pine and the birch with moss around the roots. When I was a child, before Riding Mountain became a National Park, we used to go every summer to the cottage my father and my uncle had built on Clear Lake. One summer my great-aunt Ett accompanied us. She was my grandfather Wemyss' sister, a tiny dynamic woman who spoke with such a thick Scots' burr that I was never able to understand a single word she uttered. But her reaction to Clear Lake was in some way translated and communicated even to me. It was the closest thing to Scotland, she said, that she had ever seen. Perhaps some kind of ironic historical wheel had now come full circle. The Highlands of Scotland struck a chord in me because they reminded me of Clear Lake in Manitoba.

History, as history, is moving when one catches a momentary sense of it, as I think I did in the Highlands, because the humans who lived before oneself are suddenly endowed with flesh and bones, and because man's incredible ability to survive both the outer and the inner damage seems to me to be heartening wherever it occurs. But there is another kind of history, the kind that has the most power over us in unsuspected ways, the names or tunes or trees that can recall a thousand images, and this almost-family history can be related only to one's first home.

I am inclined to think that one's real roots do not extend very far back in time, nor very far forward. I can imagine and care about my possible grandchildren, and even (although in a weakened way) about my great-grandchildren. Going back, no one past my great-grandparents has any personal reality for me. I care about the ancestral past very much, but in a kind of mythical way. The ancestors, in the end, become everyone's ancestors. But the history that one can feel personally encompasses only a very few generations.

So, finally, the mock Scots retain as much emotional hold on me as the real Scots, because of very specific things—the daft and un-named bird on our plaid pin, and my grandmother singing "I love a lassie, a bonnie Highland lassie, she's as fair as the lily in the dell." These things are genuinely mine. They don't relate to Scotland any more than the transplanted names do, at least for me, and they don't need to. I know where they belong.

I lived in Toronto for the academic year of 1969–70, as writer-in-residence at the University of Toronto, and acquired a cottage on the Otonabee River, near Peterborough, during that period. When I wrote about Lakefield in this article, I didn't imagine that within a few years one of its old brick houses would be mine and that I would be settled in a small town not unlike the one in which I grew up. In preparing this collection, I was tempted to expand this article and to include some of the things I have since learned and come to feel about this area, but I decided not to do so, and to leave my first impressions intact.

Down East

My geographical grasp of Canada was not learned at school. It came straight from the semantic roots of what I now perceive to have been my folk culture, and it was many years before I suspected that in text-book terms it might not be totally accurate. It was, however, very accurate psychologically. A quick glance at the geographical terminology of my youth will reveal my prairie origins.

The West, of course, meant us, that is, the three prairie provinces, especially Manitoba and Saskatchewan. Alberta just barely qualified—it was a little too close to those mountains for our entire trust. We sometimes suspected that Albertans had more in common with *The Coast* than they did with us. *The Coast* meant only one thing—British Columbia. As far as we were concerned, there was only one coast. The eastern coast, presumably, was so distant as to be beyond our ken. *The Coast* was a kind of Lotus Land which we half scorned and half envied. All prairie people, as was well known, wanted to retire there. Think of it—a land with no winter, semi-tropical beaches, breezes which were invariably balmy; a land where the apricots and apples virtually dropped into your mouth. Jerusalem the Golden, with milk and honey blest— that was how we thought of it. At the same time we considered in our puritanical hearts that our climate was healthier, as we sneezed our way through the desperate winter and thawed our white-frozen ears and knees gently, not too close to the stove, as we had been taught.

Apart from *The West* and *The Coast*, our country contained only one other habitable area (*The North*, in our innocent view, being habitable only by the indigenous Eskimo and the occasional mad trapper), and that was *Down East*. This really meant Ontario. Quebec and the Maritimes existed in geography books but not in our imaginations, a sad lack in the teaching of Canadian literature, I now think, being partly responsible. Everyone born on the prairies has a sense of distance, but there were limitations even to our horizon-accustomed eyes. *Down East* was within our scope, and upon it we foisted our drought-and-depression fantasies. The people *Down East* did not know what it meant to be hard up—like most depressed areas, we had the illusion of solitary suffering. I did not personally suffer very much, if at all, from the depression of the thirties, but I certainly imbibed the dominant myths of my culture. *Down East* was mainly composed of banks and mortgage companies, and the principal occupation of most Ontario people was grinding the faces of the poor. In their spare time, they attended cocktail parties and made light scornful banter of their impoverished relatives out west. My only relative *Down East* was an aunt married to a man who had once, glamorously, been a bush pilot, but of course that was different. This same aunt told me not long ago that she lived in Ontario for years before the prairie chip finally fell from her shoulders.

As the years passed, I grew to understand that my early impressions of Ontario were somewhat distorted, to put it mildly. But something of the old antagonism towards Upper Canada remained until the past year when I lived there and discovered something of Ontario for the first time.

Yes, there were many things I didn't like, chief among them the virtually cannibalistic advance of what we are pleased to term, with stunning inaccuracy, Progress. Toronto, it is true, has more banks than even I dreamed possible in my youthful condemnation, and one has to drive seemingly endless miles even to begin to get away from the loathsome high-rise apartments going up everywhere. Yes, you listen to the radio in the morning and hear the city's air-pollution index and wonder if you should venture as far as Yonge and Bloor without a gas mask. Yes, water pollution wades deeper and deeper into the Great Lakes. But there are other areas still left, and one prays for their survival.

The land around Bancroft in the fall. I had never seen the hardwood maples in autumn before. The prairie maples turn yellow, marvellously clear and clean-coloured. But these scarlet flames of trees, a shouting of pure colour like some proclamation of glory, have to be seen to be believed. Words won't make a net to catch that picture; nor, I think, will paint. But suddenly I could see why the Group of

Seven was so obsessed with trying to get it down, this incredible splendour, and why, for so long, many Canadian writers couldn't see the people for the trees. With trees like these, no wonder humans felt overwhelmed. The maples stretched along ridge after ridge, with yellow poplar and speared pine for the eye's variety, as though God had planned it this way. A friend and I walked over the clumps of coarse grass, over the slabs of exposed bronze-brown rock, and there in the small valley was a beaver lake, the camouflaged lodges barely discernible, and only the wind and the birds to be heard, the cold air gold with sun and azure with sky.

"This is my heartland," my friend said, simply and without embarrassment. She did not visualize herself as a wordsmith, yet when she talked about the country around Bancroft, she enabled me to see beyond the trees to the roots which exist always within the minds of humans. Her people farmed this land for generations. Cousins and uncles still lived here, in the farmhouses half hidden away from the gravel or dirt roads. I began to realize that most of the prairie towns and farms I remembered were in fact relatively new compared with this part of the land.

Later, months later, thinking of the blazing cold conflagration of the maples in fall, and the sense of history, of ancestors buried here, I thought of one of Margaret Atwood's poems about Susanna Moodie, when that prickly, over-proud pioneer lady's son was drowned. The last line of one poem will always haunt the mind—"I planted him in this country like a flag."

Kitchener and/or Waterloo. I never did discover which part of the town was which, or what to call each. Two towns have merged, but both seem to main-

tain their separate identities. This is Mennonite country, and in the markets on weekends you can buy
homemade sausage and cheese. I visited a friend who
has lived there most of her life, and who writes about
the Mennonite people, their customs, their cooking,
and, more than anything, their life-view, which is to
us amazingly untouched by this century, amazingly
simple and related to one another. Naturally, outsiders tend to regard their way of life as archaic, but
sometimes one wonders if their view won't endure
longer than ours.

Morning came early in the country just outside
Kitchener, and I got up despite my hatred of early
rising, drawn by the sun on the snow. I tramped along
the paths beside Sunfish Lake, thinking that people in
Canada really ought to be told that not everywhere
does the winter come like this, with this brightness of
both air and snow. Through the woods, tangled in
among the bushes, a small river tried to take its course,
and flowed despite the ice, making bizarre carvings on
the frozen parts of itself. Back at the house, looking
out the window, I saw a whole contingent of red
cardinals, coming for the birdseed my friend put out.
Arrogant crimson feathers, sleek against the snow. I
never imagined that I would be much of a bird-
watcher. But there are moments when one is struck
with a sudden intense awareness of the beauty of
creatures, and wishes their continuance could be guar-
anteed. I would like my grandchildren, when they
exist, to be able to see cardinals like these.

Peterborough. To me, this small city on the Otonabee
River meant Robertson Davies' country—some of his
books, *The Diary of Samuel Marchbanks* and others,
and himself those years ago as the fiery editor of *The*

Peterborough Examiner. The area remains so related, but now I see it as the historical home of Susanna Moodie as well, that snobbish composer of dreadful patriotic poems and writer of *Roughing It in the Bush*, that genteel and self-dramatizing English lady who never really came to terms with what was a very raw land when she settled here in the 1830's. More especially the area now evokes Catharine Parr Traill, who made this land her own, who named many of the wildflowers, and who lived hereabouts until she died at a very old age—a woman both gentle and strong.

Many of the Peterborough streets are maple-edged, and the old houses are square, solid, dignified, red-brick, some with wooden lacework around their elegant verandas. The houses sit in the shade of their trees, cogitating on the past, which in some cases is more than a century. Not long for Europe, but long enough in our terms. These streets do seem to be from another era. One almost expects little kids in knicker-bockers or frilly gingham gowns to spring out of the next hedge with homemade stands and one-cent lemonade signs.

In nearby Lakefield, you can buy pine blanket chests made by someone's great-grandfather, and if you're lucky you can hear an old-timer reminiscing about the last of the great paddlewheel steamers that used to ply these waters. In Lakefield, too, they make excellent cheese. You can buy it, in three degrees of sharpness, from the place where it is produced, and the giant cheese wheels smell and taste like your childhood. There is also a place where they still make their own ice-cream, in a dozen flavours.

Taking a taxi in Peterborough is a very different

matter from taking a taxi in Toronto. In the city, the cab drivers are fluently and instantly conversational, a motley collection of men from nearly all corners of the earth. In Peterborough, when they get to know you a little, then they talk. Most seem to be local men. When they talk over the intercom, it is to people who are their known neighbours. They do not, as in Toronto, say, "Come in, Number 87654321." They say, "Hey, Ron, where the heck *are* you?" Sometimes a despatcher loses his temper and addresses a particular driver as "sir." "Well, sir, if you can't find that address on Charlotte Street, you've got to have been born yesterday." I listened to these exchanges for quite some time before it dawned on me that "sir" in these parts could sometimes mean an ironic reproach. A legacy, perhaps, from the hordes of bloody-minded Irish who settled this area? The well-driller who divined with a willow wand (yes, it really works) the well for my cottage near Peterborough, also had an inflection of those Irish. When asked about the well's potential, he replied, "Lard, woman, you got enough water there to supply halfa Trona." And I was reminded of James Joyce—"Hail Mary, full of grease, the Lard is with thee. . . ."

Probably I will be accused of sentimentality and nostalgia, writing affectionately about these towns *Down East* and this countryside, but I don't think this accusation would be entirely true. No era that is gone can ever return, nor would one want it to. I will, however, admit that in looking at towns where some quietness and sense of history remain I am looking at them at least partly as a tourist. I'm aware that under the easily perceivable surface there lurk the same old demons of malice and man's persistent misunderstanding of man. I was born in a small town—I *know* all that. But I would venture to suggest my own theory about such places.

Are they really anachronisms? Or may they possibly turn out to be to our culture what the possession of manuscripts in monasteries was to mediaeval Europe during the dark ages? Maybe some of them will survive, and maybe we will need them. Whatever their limitations, it is really only in communities such as these that the individual is known, assessed, valued, seen, and can breathe without battling for air. They may not be our past so much as our future, if we have one.

This article was published in 1972. In the intervening years, I've had further adventures with the people of The Box, most of them happy episodes despite my perpetual nervousness at such times. Possibly the most exciting TV coverage I've had in recent years wasn't focused on me at all, although I was there and it wouldn't have taken place without the existence of a book of mine. It occurred at the launching party for *The Diviners*, when a divining contest was held at the Science Centre in Toronto. A real diviner had been found some time earlier, by my publishers, and he had kindly agreed to find several water courses and to bury a marker at their junction. Willow wands were provided, and prizes offered to those three persons who came closest to finding the junction of the underground water courses. The contest was open to the public. The TV crews turned up in strength, most of them rather sceptical. And lo and behold—no less than seven experienced diviners, four men and three women, came in from small Ontario towns, to show their skill. That was a splendid moment, when all those divining wands began magically turning within those hands. Only one member of the assembled company, apart from the seven diviners, turned out to have the gift, and that was Helen Hutchison, the TV interviewer. I saw the episode later, on the news, myself hovering gleefully in the background. It's the only time I've ever looked at myself on TV.

Inside the Idiot Box

Fate has not, thank goodness, decreed that I should spend much of my life in random appearances on television. I cannot, therefore, claim to have an intimate knowledge of the medium. Nonetheless, I have had

one or two memorable—if not, indeed, soul-shattering
—encounters with the inside of the goggle box.

I have only to conjure up in my mind's eye a TV
studio, and instantly the sweating palms and knocking
knees syndrome comes into operation. Those studios
are always cavernously gloomy, really ghostly away
out there behind the white-hot lights focused on one's
all-too-inadequate face and form.

Can lights be said to be *shrill?* Those lights are. They
shriek, and the message is plain—one is going to make
a total fool of oneself, and will undoubtedly cringe
at the memory forevermore. The only solution to this
situation is calculated nonchalance. You don't *care* if
you make a fool of yourself. It matters not, in the
eternal scheme of things.

My initiation into the dark mysteries of The Box
came shortly after my first novel was published. Three
or four people were to be interviewed, ten minutes
each. We sat with puppet-like obedience in an ante-
room, awaiting our turn. I was perspiring freely and
shaking all over as though with palsy. The woman
beside me began to chat. It was not until that moment
that I truly knew what the phrase "Job's comforter"
meant.

"I've been on this kind of show so often it's getting
boring," she admitted modestly. "The real trick, of
course, is never to look at the monitor—you know,
the TV set that's sitting in front of you. Many's the
time I've seen a person crack up—actually go right to
pieces—just because they looked at the monitor and
saw themselves there."

This I could easily understand. I could visualize
myself, staring at my own image, probably stopping

talking in order to listen to what that other Me was going to say next.

"But that's not all," my cheery companion went on. "Lots of other things can put a person off, if they're inexperienced. Like getting a dumb interviewer. Or one who talks too fast, so you miss the question. You learn to improvise, but that's hardly possible for people who've never done it before."

She then leaned closer to me.

"This your first time, dear?" she said.

My second appearance on the merciless screen, at about the same time, was even worse. They were trying out applicants for a new talk show, and the glamorous young woman who was interviewing me had never done an interview before. I was, so to speak, her guinea pig. She also hadn't read my novel, as she confessed brightly beforehand.

It was with deeply sinking heart that I shuffled into the studio, a lamb to the slaughter. Then we were ON, and furthermore, it was live. She began to question me about Africa, the setting for my novel. To say the interview was painful would be a miracle of understatement. But the ending was the clincher.

"Tell me, Mrs. Laurence," she said in dulcet tones, "do you think Africa would be a better place if there were more people like yourself there?"

The end. I had no time to pick up the pieces. The scene began to swim before my eyes. If I could have fainted, I would assuredly have done so.

My publisher, Jack McClelland, had been watching the show at his home.

"Funniest thing I ever saw," he told me later. "The camera panned in beautifully to a last shot of you with your mouth falling open about a mile wide and a look of complete horror on your face."

Some years later, the summer my novel *A Jest of God* was published, I went across Canada on what I had planned as a holiday.

"*We* think of it," McClelland said grimly, "as a working trip."

And so it was. My publishers, God bless them, had arranged for interviews everywhere. I felt like a campaigning politician. It was in the course of this trip that I learned something of the devious ploys used by television personnel.

"That was just great," the interviewer said, in Montreal, after the ordeal was over.

"You really think so?" I said eagerly and, as I realized later, naively.

"Certainly. You can always tell by the way the sound technicians react. If they're interested, the show is going great. Jimmy and Ron, there, were listening to every word."

On to Toronto.

"That was just great," the interviewer said, after the ordeal was over.

"You really think so?" I said, somewhat less enthusiastically this time.

"Certainly. You can always tell by the way the sound technicians react. If they're interested, the show is going great. Peter and George, there, were listening to every word."

By the time I got to Vancouver, I simply said "Marvelous," tiredly, when I was told it had been just great. Let's face it—the sound technicians probably couldn't care less, in most cases, whether you're babbling pompously on about the literary symbolism in mail-order catalogues or chirpily reciting the cute saying of your little kids. What really grabs them is *sounds*, not words. As long as your voice doesn't quaver or shift from soprano to bass, and the palpitations of your panic-stricken heart aren't being picked up by that mike concealed amongst your upper underwear, they're ecstatic.

The first time a TV crew ever came to my house in England was, as it happened, in the dead of winter. My house does not have central heating. My study, where we were filming, is heated electrically and there is only one wall plug, into which the TV lights had to be plugged. The heater, therefore, was off. As always, it took what seemed like hours to get everything set up and ready to go.

By this time, the Canadian interviewer's opinion of England in general and my house in particular was in a state of sharp decline. All I can say is that it's lucky the film wasn't in colour. We were all bright blue with cold.

The most fun I've ever had in connection with The Box was the occasion last summer when a TV team from Winnipeg visited the cabin where I was living in southern Ontario. There was Don, the producer, Pat, assistant and Girl Friday, Cliff, the sound technician, and another Don, whom I shall call Don Two, the cameraman. Don One decided it would be better to film outside, so Don Two got the camera set up, and Cliff arranged his complex recording equipment. Don One was to interview me, and then we'd do a few shots for background.

I steeled myself. Right. We were ready. Pat held up

the board with the show's name and made her short announcement. She then clacked the sign for Take One—a gesture which has always somehow struck me as hilarious—and leapt out of camera range like a startled fawn. I was finding it difficult not to laugh, but I summoned such seriousness as I could and began responding to Don's first question.

At that precise second the air was filled with hideous sounds coming from across the river. Every chainsaw in southern Ontario was apparently giving voice like a giant pack of baying hounds and belling beagles. They whined. They screeched. They rumbled and roared. We were utterly silenced.

We waited. The chainsaws continued. Obviously they intended to go on all day. We tried going inside the shack, but it was no better there. Cliff said he thought he could adjust the recording equipment so it would cut out most of the noise. He tinkered with knobs and dials and electronic marvels and finally announced that it was okay. We could go on. By this time, no one was certain we could carry through without punctuating the procedure with unacceptable guffaws.

On such occasions, however, the adrenaline pours into the blood, the spine stiffens and you find ultimately that the thing is over and you've all got through it somehow. We relaxed for a while, or at least most of us did. Sound technicians' ears are not like most people's ears. They really *hear* things, those guys. The chainsaws had blessedly decided to knock off, so Cliff wandered around with a dreamy expression on his face, recording birdsong, bees, the wind in the leaves, the far-off mutter of an outboard motor.

"Okay, now for the background shots," Don One said finally. "Can you pretend you're coming back from a walk? You know. Saunter around. Pick a flower."

"Pick a flower?"

"Sure. One of those in that clump down by the river. That'd look good."

So I began strolling to and fro, while Don Two followed me with a hand-held camera. I walked slowly to the end of my dock, resisting the temptation to leap dramatically into the water. It occurred to me that this sort of promenade would be easier to accomplish with aplomb if one had been twenty-one and looked like Miss World.

I turned back towards the cabin and mentally chose the flower I was about to pluck gracefully. I thought that the tall stalk covered with yellow blossoms would show up well on film. By now I was beginning rather to enjoy all this. Small fantasies were playing in the theatre of my mind. Me, communing with the great outdoors, gently picking a posy with which to decorate my simple cedar abode. That kind of thing.

I leaned over the flower and grasped the stem delicately. I snapped it—or at least I intended to snap it. Nothing happened. I pulled a little more strongly. No go. That flower wasn't giving up without a tussle. I became agitated and before I knew what I was doing, I found myself grabbing the wretched plant with both hands and wrestling with it. It won. It bent a little but it refused to break. Don Two, doubled over with laughter, had long since abandoned filming the scene. Perhaps he should have stayed with it. I might have rivalled Laurel and Hardy. On second thought, fighting with a *flower*—well, maybe that's going too far.

"I think," Don One said with admirable tact, "we had better try that one again."

The next time I picked a wild aster. It was tiny, weak and weedy, and I knew I could best it. I later learned from my wildflower book that my yellow-blossomed antagonist was a Great Mullein of the Figwort family. With a chivalric name like that, no wonder it was prepared to put up such a gallant challenge.

In the days of my first TV encounter, some ten years ago, great gobs of gooey and violently tinted makeup used to be applied to the face, thus making the temporary performer feel even more like an amateur clown who has stumbled unwittingly into a circus of accomplished tightrope walkers. This is no longer done, which is a help. Live shows, too, are pretty rare now, it seems to me, and this also is a blessing to such as myself, whose nerves tend to be constructed of gelatine. Why have I appeared at all, if it scares me as much as I maintain it does? Well, that's an awkward question.

I suppose, partly, it seems churlish to say no. After all, they've got to fill the talk shows with *someone*, even if it's only the occasional writer or so, which is really scraping the bottom of the barrel. I suppose, also, there remains the faint if misguided hope that it may help the books. TV interviews, like parties, are okay for writers provided they don't get to be a habit.

"I watched your interview last night. What did you think of it?"

I've been asked this question a number of times, and it poses no problem for me. I can reply honestly that I don't know. While not the greatest TV fan in the entire world, there are moments when I'll watch nearly anything on The Box. With one exception. The one performance I've never been able to bring myself to watch is my own. That way, I always feel, would lie madness.

Since this article was written in 1970, my experience of taxis has increased tenfold. In the summers, the taxi in my village collects me at my cottage each week and brings me home, a distance of some twenty miles. I do my shopping, collect my mail, and return to the cottage by taxi. Some people consider me wildly extravagant until I ask them how much it costs them to buy, insure, and run a car. Taxi-takers of the world, unite.

I Am a Taxi

A small but poignant joke, of which I am bizarrely fond, concerns a gentleman who was struck by a motor vehicle at the corner of Bloor and Yonge in the city of Toronto. Dazed, bruised, and bleeding, but still conscious, he crawled to the sidewalk, where a young man was standing. "Quick!" gasped the injured man. "Call me a taxi!" The youth looked down and shrugged. "So okay," he said, "you're a taxi."

Apart from its pertinent commentary on contemporary urban life, I like this joke because its punch line could be applied perfectly seriously to me. Part of my mind is definitely labelled *Taxi*, for the sufficient reason that I have taken so many cabs in my peregrinations throughout cities in various parts of the world that in some way I identify with cabs. I collect taxis and the life stories of taxi drivers in precisely the same way as taxis themselves collect a multitudinous variety of—as I believe they are known in the trade—fares. (I have always rather resented being referred to as a "fare," which seems to me a crass denial of individuality, but let it pass.)

I've taken taxis in Vancouver, where all they complain about is the inadequacy of the Lions' Gate Bridge. In other parts of the world, the opening gambit of most taxi conversations concerns the weather; in Vancouver it concerns The Bridge and to what extent it is impassable at this moment.

I've taken taxis in Athens, where it does no good to produce the Greek Tourist Bureau map of the city —the street names are all in Roman lettering, and the cab driver only understands Greek lettering. Furthermore, his natural pride is offended by seeing the street names of his beloved city set down incomprehensibly in alien symbols. He will shake his head courteously, give you one brief fiery glare of rage, and drive away. The answer is simple but cunning. You get someone —the travel agent, or the hotel manager—to write down in Greek lettering all the place names which could conceivably interest you, so that all you have to do is produce your list and point.

I've taken taxis in Cairo, where every cab appears to be held together with elastic bands and patched up with chewing gum, and where the drivers have a splendidly fatalistic Muslim *élan*—if Allah means us to die, we'll die, so why worry?

I once took a taxi forty miles through an Easter blizzard in the Black Isle of Ross-shire, in northern Scotland, from Cromarty to Inverness, to convey my son to hospital when he'd fallen ill while on holiday. I was regaled the whole way by gruesome stories from the Highland driver, all about the other cases he'd rushed into hospital throughout the years—desperate delays at the ferry; screaming women giving birth in the back seat; perforated ulcers; burst appendixes; all sorts of jolly stuff, calculated to soothe the nerves of any frantic mum.

Of all the taxis I've ever taken, the London ones are absolutely the most admirable. These English drivers are made to undergo an apprenticeship of some two years, during the first stages of which they *bicycle* around London, in order to familiarize themselves with the routes. In many years of taxi voyaging through the incredible maze of London's streets, I have only ever once encountered a cab driver who didn't know exactly how to get where I wanted to go, and that was a West End driver going into the labyrinth of Hampstead, who finally said, "Look, ducks, I'll drop you here and get you a Hampstead driver." London cab drivers are a breed apart, and my regard for them is boundless.

Among the taxis I've collected in recent years, however, undoubtedly the cheeriest ones have been in Toronto. Toronto cab drivers get my Medal of Acclaim and Approval for being the gabbiest drivers anywhere. *What?* In *Toronto*, long thought of as the last stronghold of apparently tongue-tied WASPS? Well, that was the old Toronto. This is the new. Many worthwhile hours have I spent in deep converse with the men who drive cabs in Toronto, for they are almost certainly the most highly verbal in the entire world. Even the ones whose mother-tongue is not English are verbal.

The young man has high Slavic cheekbones, hair the colour of August-bleached grass, and an accent I can't place. I make my standard remarks about the awfulness of the traffic, just to get things going.

"I drive cab during the day," he volunteers. "At night I go to school."

Oh? Where? And what is he taking?

"I am taking accountancy. I was accountant in my own country, that is Yugoslavia. Then they tell me I have to go in the army. Being accountant—that is not so exciting job, you think? You are wrong. It is all right. My own time is my own. But army—not for me. I stay six months. Then I run away."

He finally worked his way over to Canada, two years ago. He knew no English at that time, but his English is pretty fair now. His problem is that he misses Yugoslavia, which in his eyes is ten times more attractive than Canada, geographically, but he can't return or he'll be nabbed. His mother still lives there, and he would like to bring her to Canada, but she doesn't want to come. His father died in the last war, and this boy cannot believe that he died with purpose. A common enough story, I suppose, but what is uncommon is his optimism. He doesn't think that Canada is the promised land—he merely intends to find out how to live reasonably well here, and somehow one is convinced that he will do that, according to his own lights.

"My girl—she don't like me driving cab," he grins. "But I tell her—wait, wait. Maybe she will."

He's not after short-term rewards, and whether or not his goals are admirable, who knows? But he's not going to change them, and poor girl if she doesn't see that.

Another time, another driver. He is small, wiry, jittery to a degree, greying hair, hands which clutch the steering wheel too tightly.

"You know something?" he says. "This goddamn traffic is getting me down. I been driving a cab in this city for fourteen years, and I never thought I'd see the day when I could say the traffic was getting me down. But there it is. I got a wife, two kids at college, the house isn't any palace but it's okay, and all of them think everything's just fine. But me, I get up in the mornings and I think—holy jesus, another day I got to sit quiet and not flip my lid when some of these crazy buggers cut in ahead of you like it was going to save them hours, but you know what? They don't gain nothing. Nothing. Silly bastard! See that? Now, how much time is he gonna save by doing that? One minute? And he coulda piled into me . . ."

It is not a good business to be in, if you've lost your nerve.

I arrive back in Toronto from New York, and the cab driver is a West Indian. I can't wait to get all my feelings about the deadly city off my mind. New York, I say, has to be seen to be believed. It's terrifying. Try to get a cab outside Grand Central Station on a Saturday night and you feel you're not real. If you had a heart attack, they'd walk over you and hardly notice the blood on their shoes.

"Man, lady, I know," he says with feeling. "My own sister live in New York. I was down to see her last year. I been living here in Toronto for five years and this ain't heaven, take it from me. But I go to New York, and there's my sister's apartment—man, I'm not joking you, it's got six locks on the door. This key, that key, you turn all of them keys this way and that, a hundred times, and you in, finally, if you lucky. 'How can you live this way?' I ask her. 'Listen,' she says to me, 'I live this way or I dead.' There you got it."

Sooner or later, one is bound to meet a cab driver from the same part of the world as you hail from yourself. This guy, although not from a prairie town as I myself am, comes originally from North Winnipeg, my old stamping-ground many years ago. He, like me, lived near Selkirk Avenue, and if you've never shopped on Selkirk Avenue on a weekend, you haven't lived. We discuss all the groceries and markets we used to know. *Hey, you remember—Why, sure*—In his Winnipeg voice he tells me he speaks French, Russian, and Yiddish as well as English. Also, he claims to have thirteen daughters and a son.

"If you don't believe me," he says breezily, "you don't believe in God."

We zoom up Avenue Road.

"You see that apartment block?" he asks gravely.

"Yeh?"

"I don't own it," he says.

A different kettle of fish, quite literally, is the cab driver from Newfoundland. Newfoundlanders do laugh a lot when among themselves. But this one is morose and brooding. He is shy, small, tough as old boots probably, and has a kind of accent that one would never place as Canadian, for the Newfoundland speech is not like anyone else's. A soft, rather melodic voice, with undertones of—what? Ireland, Cornwall, perhaps even the lost rhythms and accents of Elizabethan English. It is hard to get talk going, but it is a long drive that evening to a friend's house, so ultimately he opens up. He is so homesick for his rocky island that he can hardly bear it.

"I send the kids and the wife back every summer," he says, "and I go myself if I can afford it. Life is different there, you know. Very different. I can go back to the place where I was born, now, and maybe I've been away for a year or so, but if it was ten years it would be the same. I walk down the street and everybody knows me, you see. They say, 'Here's John Sykes' son, come home.' It's not the same anywhere else. Nobody knows you here."

Why does he stay in Toronto, I ask. Why not go back?

"I can do better for my kids here," he says bleakly. "I can earn more."

Do better in what ways, one wonders.

Or the cab driver from Hong Kong. Smiling, full of quips. He's been here for seven years. Before that he was in San Francisco and then Vancouver. He was born in China. He is forty-odd, and all his near family either died in China at the time of the revolution (he does not say on which side, and what does it now matter?) or are making paper flowers and blown-together kids' clothes for Hong Kong export.

"I don't care," he says, laughing with careful gaiety. "That is the only way to live—not to care. Toronto fine. Same as anywhere else. I don't really care about anything much. That the only way to live."

Oddly sad and unreachable, this Chinese Pagliacci. And yet the rules which he has had to evolve have worked. For "live" read "survive."

Some of the best and truest drivers, those who unerringly know the way and who talk the easiest, are Torontonians, naturally. For them, the intricate crescents of Rosedale present no problems, and their humour is peculiarly their own. They are of this city; they belong here. They are a pleasure to talk with.

"You know how often a fare gets in the front seat?" he says, smiling with cool raised eyebrows into the car mirror. "Like, never, hardly. So this nice-looking doll climbs in the front seat. Well, that's okay by me. But when I take my wife out, weekends, see, if ever I have to brake sudden, I throw an arm across her so's she won't jolt forward. Living seatbelt, that's me. So some lunatic cuts in front of me when this doll is in the front seat, and I'm braking—*kapow!* And automatically I throw my arm across her to protect her, only of course it lands right across her breasts. So is she grateful? Hell, she thinks I'm making a pass. How can you win?"

There are, I've decided, two kinds of people in this world. Those who habitually take taxis and those who don't. You really know you're one of the former when it happens, as it did a short time ago to me in Toronto, that you are explaining where you live. "It's between Avenue Road and Bathurst, just below Lawrence."

"It's okay, dear," the driver says. "I know where you live, from the last time I took you home."

Alas, I hadn't remembered him. I guess that was one guy whose life story I didn't get to hear. Maybe next time.

Since this article was published in 1972, I have received and written thousands more letters. The letters accusing me of various dreadful lapses from respectability have been, I am happy to say, very much in a minority. Some of them have, however, been fairly memorable. One said that *The Happy Hooker*, not my novel *The Diviners*, should have got the Governor General's Award—at least the H.H. wasn't *blasphemous*. I thought she must have read a different novel to the one I wrote. Another, also referring to *The Diviners*, proceeded to outline the correspondent's life history in some four or five pages, and then went on to say "I'm really writing to tell you how much I hate your novel." Yet another claimed that what she called "a knowledge of the seamier side of life" did nothing to "further healthy thought patterns." I was reminded of the words to the song of Lazarus, in the novel: "What made him walk so slow/Well, they didn't care to know/It was easier by far to look away." The majority of letters which I've received in the last few years, though, have been incredibly heartening to me —letters from women and men, saying they had read *The Diviners* and that it had spoken to their own lives. I haven't been able to answer all these letters; time just didn't permit it. So I'd like to say here how very much they have meant to me, and how grateful I am for them.

Living Dangerously . . . by Mail

I am an inveterate letter writer. I must write thousands every year, and sometimes I get the feeling that my typewriter, in the letter-writing context, is not so much a typewriter as a kind of radio transmitter through which I send out my messages and moans to friends, or my arguments and appeals to publishers.

I am also an addicted receiver of letters. I'm hooked on the things.

In the morning, if the postman is late, I become jittery and tend to pace the floor nervously until I hear the familiar *thwack* of the mail arriving in my letterbox. If the postman passes by the house, I have severe withdrawal symptoms—depression, anxiety, and so on. Are my friends angry with me for some unknown reason? Have they all suddenly been stricken with a mysterious plague? Then the next day six letters arrive, and I sigh with relief, my habit supported once more.

Most of the letters I've received throughout the years have been of a fairly reassuring or at any rate friendly nature. Letters from other writers, telling me of the horrible battles they're bravely enduring with their current novel or poems, and sympathizing with my airletterborne howls of panic, self-pity, and dramatic suffering over my own writing. Much-needed letters from my dearest friend and fellow novelist saying, "Courage—Forward!" Letters from my publishers, discussing a completed manuscript or offering encouragement over an uncompleted one. Letters from friends and family, keeping in contact. And even, sometimes, letters from people telling me they've enjoyed one of my books.

Where correspondence is concerned, I cannot legitimately complain and indeed am *not* complaining. Really.

Nevertheless—

There is another and somewhat kinky side to my correspondence. The dark side, you might say, of the moon. The other side of the coin. The skeleton in the

closet. The worm in the apple. The fly in the oint-
ment. (Where did *that* phrase ever come from, by the
way? Fly in the beer or the fruit salad would make
more sense.)

These other letters occasionally give me the sense
of inhabiting a whole different and faintly sinister
dimension, or, at the very least, of living dangerously
by mail. I once received one of those chain letters
which said that if I did not immediately send off
copies of same to about a thousand friends, something
exceedingly nasty and overpoweringly unlucky would
happen to me. I was not about to be conned, but all
the same my image in the mirror for some days showed
me the haunted face of one who knows she is living
at the very edge of the precipice.

The terrible thing was that I had posted the manuscript of a novel the same day I received the unpleasant epistle. Like most writers, I am as supersti-
tious as a caveman or an actor. I was convinced that
I would receive a reply from my publishers telling
me this was the most boring and totally disastrous
novel they'd ever read.

Then there was the lady who wrote to me about
my first novel, *This Side Jordan*. This was my first
anti-fan letter, and it drew a certain amount of psychic
blood from me.

"I have never read such a disgusting book as yours,"
she charmingly stated, "and I would as soon allow my
young friends to handle a snake as your novel."

Fine piece of Freudian imagery there, I thought.
She went on to say that she wondered why I had been
compelled to write a novel full of such obscenities as
chamber-pots. I also wondered, in astonishment, so I

checked through the book. As I had thought, the offending china object was mentioned only once. She certainly hadn't missed it. She ended by advising me to "look up and see the angel."

I recalled this letter a few years later, when I'd written my second novel, because strangely enough I *had* looked up and seen *The Stone Angel.* I have a feeling, though, that the irascible and steel-spined old Hagar in the novel was possibly not quite what the chastising lady had in mind.

The Stone Angel brought me a number of letters which I found very heartening. It also brought in a few which had a certain wry (if unintended) humour.

"Could you tell me," one letter seriously said, "where you did your geriatric research?"

Another and much-cherished document said, "*The Stone Angel* is the most telling argument for euthanasia I have ever read."

By the time my novels *A Jest of God* and *The Fire-Dwellers* were published, I had become considerably more thick-skinned about the odd reader (odd in both senses, if you ask me) who appeared to believe that mine was a lifetime devoted to the propagation of hard-core pornography. Even so, I have to admit I was a little startled by the good lady who began her letter by telling me how much she admired my writing and proceeded to comment thusly, complete with spelling error in the second title:

"In The Fire-Dwellers—was all that swearing really necessary? The rest of the world will think the average Canadian housewife is nothing but a guttersnipe! Then A Gest of God (I don't know why you have your characters blaming *Him* for everything when they don't believe in Him!) Now I'm deep in Stone Angel (Hagar—what a name for a girl!) You really are getting mileage out of MANAWAKA!! But don't any of the people recognize themselves in it?"

Oh well. I forbore from telling her that the people in my own real hometown could scarcely have recognized themselves in the novel, for the simple reason that they weren't in it. Fiction *does* exist, despite murmurings to the contrary. And if I was getting mileage out of Manawaka—well, tough beans, lady, it's *my* town; it exists in the mind and on the page, but you won't find it on any of the maps in the geography books. I also forbore from telling her that the rest of the world wasn't really going to be all that uptight about the occasional expletive in a Canadian novel.

Another aspect of my worm-in-the-apple or fly-in-the-beer correspondence is somewhat more personally involving. Namely, those written wrangles which I have had with various publishers over my writing. All have ultimately, I am glad to say, ended in amicable fashion. But at the time some of these communications, both theirs and mine, have given rise to the thought that here in my quiet country life I am living in almost too risky and adventurous a manner, albeit vicariously by mail.

When my first novel was accepted, one of my publishers sent me extracts from their readers' reports. They hardly ever did this, they informed me, but in this case they thought I could take it. They must indeed have believed me strong in the psyche. What one of the publisher's readers had said was that he was "only reasonably nauseated" by the oratorical nature of much of the inner monologue in the novel.

For days I alternated between rage and total defeat. Then I got out the manuscript and realized that the reader had been right. I went back into the novel and weeded out a great deal, and lived to bless the gent with the uncertain digestion.

I've had many exchanges with publishers, and very often an editor's advice has resulted in a better book. I don't regard anything I've written as deathless or untouchable. If an editor's comments seem true and to the point, I take his advice and try to do something about it. If I disagree, I argue, usually over-reacting but at least discovering whether I can stand behind what I've written or not, and why.

There is, however, one exception to my sweet reasonableness, one area in which I will probably fight like a tigress. The worst—or perhaps the most entertaining, in retrospect—typewritten battles I've had with publishers have been over the matter of titles. I've had more trouble with titles than a prospective peer. And I've defended my titles more often than a middleweight boxer.

A title should, if possible, be like a line of poetry—capable of saying a great deal with hardly any words. The title of a novel should in some way express the whole novel, its themes and even something of its outcome. It should all be there, in a phrase. I don't pretend my titles are perfect, but I believe they're the best ones that could have been found.

My American publishers did not like the title for my second novel, which at that time was *Hagar*. I kept getting letters from them, making helpful suggestions.

"What about calling it *Old Lady Shipley?*" they would say.

I would then hurl myself at my typewriter and yell loudly in print, "No, No, A Million Times No!" My English publishers, realizing my anxiety and knowing that I myself didn't much like *Hagar* as a title, got into the act.

"Dear Margaret—I am very interested to hear you have been re-reading the Psalms in an effort to find a title for *Hagar*. I think I have just the right title, also from Psalms. What about *Bottle in the Smoke?* You know, from the verse that says *And I am become as a bottle in the smoke—*"

A *what* in the *what*? Good grief! Once more my rueful non-acceptance flooded the mails. I sat up nights, convinced that the answer was somewhere in the Psalms. Once I thought I had it. The verse was: *As with a sword in my bones, so do mine enemies reproach me, while they say daily unto me, Where is thy God?* I bashed off letters to all three publishers.

"Great title has come to mind! *Sword in my Bones.* How about that?"

Less than an hour after I had posted these letters, I was again at the typewriter.

"*Sword in my Bones* obviously no good. Sounds like a tale of pirates and buried treasure."

Then one evening I picked up the manuscript of the novel, by now having almost given up hope of finding even a passable title. I read the first sentence. It was this: "Above the town, on the hill brow, the stone angel used to stand." The title, the real and true and only possible title had been there all the time, in the first line of the book. I wrote to the publishers and simply said, "The Stone Angel." Naturally, everyone could see it immediately. Calm after the storm.

With *The Fire-Dwellers* I had another set-to. One of my editors wrote to say that although she was enthusiastic about what she correctly called "the orchestration" in that novel, she had doubts about the title. As usual, I over-reacted ferociously.

I instantly tapped out a five-page single-space communication on my typewriter transmitter, explaining why this was the only possible title. It had connotations of things like cave-dwellers and apartment-dwellers, the two most separate poles of our existence on earth. It also related to the verse from Sandburg's *Losers* which was quoted after the title page—"I who have fiddled in a world on fire." It related, as well, to Stacey's recurring thought about the nursery rhyme —"Ladybird, ladybird, fly away home/Your house is on fire, your children are gone."

The fire theme threads through the novel, the fires being both inner and outer, and if we are to live in the present world, we must learn to live within the fires and still survive until we die. I expressed all this in what I believed at the time to be a cool restrained prose, but later saw was a letter of such passionate emotion that it was a wonder my editor could reply in the calm way she did.

Simmer down, she said in effect. Relax. We get the message. The title stands.

The great thing about these semi-swashbuckling encounters with publishers via the mails is, of course, that they do have a conclusion. Things are worked out and settled, and usually the book gains from the arguments. When, if ever, I retire from this profession I shall miss these embattled letters.

In the meantime, I never know from one day to

the next what the mail may bring. Bills or—horrors —communications from the Income Tax? Letters from friends, saying their novels have just been accepted, and hurrah all round? Letters from friends, saying they've run into mental blocks at chapter six, so please transmit instant love and sympathy and they will do the same when the need arises? Or perhaps a letter which goes into another area of Being, like the one I received once from a person who thought we might collaborate on a book, the material for which he knew intimately from personal experience. The subject was Flying Saucers.

Come on, postman. Where are you? It's 9:30 AM and I've had four cups of coffee, and you're usually here by 9:15, and you *know* I can't start work until—

When this article was published in 1974, I had spent the three previous summers at my cottage (known as The Shack), working on my novel *The Diviners*. A river such as the one here figures largely in the novel, although my cottage is totally different from the protagonist's house, and the novel is not autobiographical. The work circumstances were almost ideal—no interruptions for five days a week and, on weekends, friends coming to visit. They were allowed in despite the joke poster my Canadian publisher sent me, to encourage unremitting toil, and which is still tacked to a wall there. Under a stylized provincial coat-of-arms, it says, "No Visitors Allowed: By Order of The Government of Ontario; By Authority of J.G. McClelland, Servant & Publisher."

The Shack

The most loved place, for me, in this country has in fact been many places. It has changed throughout the years, as I and my circumstances have changed. I haven't really lost any of the best places from the past, though. I may no longer inhabit them, but they inhabit me, portions of memory, presences in the mind. One such place was my family's summer cottage at Clear Lake in Riding Mountain National Park, Manitoba. It was known to us simply as The Lake. Before the government piers and the sturdy log staircases down to the shore were put in, we used to slither with an exhilarating sense of peril down the steep homemade branch and dirt shelf-steps, through the stands of thin tall spruce and birch trees slender and graceful as girls, passing moss-hairy fallen logs and the white promise of wild strawberry blossoms, until we reached the sand and the hard bright pebbles of the beach at the edge of the cold spring-fed lake where at nights the loons still cried eerily, before too much humanshriek made them move away north.

My best place at the moment is very different, although I guess it has some of the attributes of that long-ago place. It is a small cedar cabin on the Otonabee River in southern Ontario. I've lived three summers there, writing, bird-watching, river-watching. I sometimes feel sorry for the people in speedboats who spend their weekends zinging up and down the river at about a million miles an hour. For all they're able to see, the riverbanks might just as well be green concrete and the river itself flowing with molten plastic.

Before sunup, I'm wakened by birdvoices and, I may say, birdfeet clattering and thumping on the cabin roof. Cursing only slightly, I get up *temporarily*, for the pre-dawn ritual of lighting a small fire in the old black woodstove (mornings are chilly here, even in summer) and looking out at the early river. The waters have a lovely spooky quality at this hour, entirely mist-covered, a secret meeting of river and sky.

By the time I get up to stay, the mist has vanished and the river is a clear ale-brown, shining with sun. I drink my coffee and sit looking out to the opposite shore, where the giant maples are splendidly green now and will be trees of flame in the fall of the year. Oak and ash stand among the maples, and the grey skeletons of the dead elms, gauntly beautiful even in death. At the very edge of the river, the willows are everywhere, water-related trees, magic trees, pale green in early summer, silvergreen in late summer, greengold in autumn.

I begin work, and every time I lift my eyes from the page and glance outside, it is to see some marvel or other. The joyous dance-like flight of the swallows. The orange-black flash of the orioles who nest across the river. The amazing takeoff of a red-winged blackbird, revealing like a swiftly unfolded fan the hidden scarlet in those dark wings. The flittering of the goldfinches, who always travel in domestic pairs, he gorgeous in black-patterned yellow feathers, she (alas) drabber in greenish grey-yellow.

A pair of great blue herons have their huge unwieldy nest about half a mile upriver, and although they are very shy, occasionally through the open door I hear a sudden approaching rush of air (yes, you can *hear* it) and look up quickly to see the magnificent unhurried sweep of those powerful wings. The only other birds which can move me so much are the Canada geese in their autumn migration flight, their far-off wilderness voices the harbinger of winter.

Many boats ply these waterways, and all of them are given mental gradings of merit or lack of it, by me. Standing low in the estimation of all of us along this stretch of the river are some of the big yachts, whose ego-tripping skippers don't have the courtesy to slow down in cottage areas and whose violent wakes scour out our shorelines. Ranking highest in my good books are the silent unpolluting canoes and rowboats, and next to them, the small outboard motorboats put-putting along and carrying patient fishermen, and the homemade houseboats, unspeedy and somehow cosy-looking, decorated lovingly with painted birds or flowers or gaudy abstract splodges.

In the quiet of afternoon, if no boats are around, I look out and see the half-moon leap of a fish, carp or muskie, so instantaneous that one has the impression of having seen not a fish but an arc of light.

The day moves on, and about four o'clock Linda and Susan from the nearby farm arrive. I call them the Girls of the Pony Express. Accompanied by dogs and laughter, they ride their horses into my yard, kindly bringing my mail from the rural route postbox up the road. For several summers it was Old Jack who used to drive his battered Volkswagen up to fetch the mail. He was one of the best neighbours and most remarkable men I've ever known. As a boy of eighteen, he had homesteaded a hundred miles north of Regina. Later, he'd been a skilled toolmaker with Ford. He'd travelled to South America and done many amazing things. He was a man whose life had taught him a lot of wisdom. After his much-loved wife died, he moved out here to the river, spending as short a winter as possible in Peterborough, and getting back into his cottage the first of anyone in the spring, when the river was still in flood and he could only get in and out, hazardously, by boat. I used to go out in his boat with him, late afternoons, and we would dawdle along the river, looking at the forest stretches and the open rolling farmlands and vast old barns, and at the smaller things close by, the heavy luxuriance of ferns at the water's rim, the dozens of snapping turtles with unblinking eyes, all sizes and generations of the turtle tribe, sunning themselves on the fallen logs in the river. One summer, Old Jack's eighty-fourth, he spent some time planting maple saplings on his property. A year later, when I saw him dying, it seemed to me he'd meant those trees as a kind of legacy, a declaration of faith. Those of us along the river, here, won't forget him, nor what he stood for.

After work, I go out walking and weed-inspecting. Weeds and wildflowers impress me as much as any cultivated plant. I've heard that in a year when the milkweed is plentiful, the Monarch butterflies will also be plentiful. This year the light pinkish milkweed flowers stand thick and tall, and sure enough, here are the dozens of Monarch butterflies, fluttering like dusky orange-gold angels all over the place. I can't identify as many plants as I'd like, but I'm learning. Chickweed, the ragged-leafed lambs' quarters, the purple-and-white wild phlox with its expensive-smelling free perfume, the pink and mauve wild asters, the two-toned yellow of the tiny butter-and-eggs flowers, the burnt orange of devil's paintbrush, the staunch nobility of the huge purple thistles, and, almost best of all, that long stalk covered with clusters of miniature creamy blossoms which I finally tracked down in my wildflower book—this incomparable plant bears the armorial name of the Great Mullein of the Fig-wort Family. It may not be the absolute prettiest of our wildflowers, but it certainly has the most stunning pedigree.

It is night now, and there are no lights except those of our few cottages. At sunset, an hour or so ago, I watched the sun's last flickers touching the rippling river, making it look as though some underwater world had lighted all its candles down there. Now it is dark. Dinner over, I turn out the electric lights in the cabin so I can see the stars. The black sky-dome (or perhaps skydom, like kingdom) is alive and alight.

Tomorrow the weekend will begin, and friends will arrive. We'll talk all day and probably half the night, and that will be good. But for now, I'm content to be alone, because loneliness is something that doesn't exist here.

This article was published in December 1974, just before our first Christmas in my Lakefield house, which is now establishing some of its own traditions, while as always carrying over some of those from the past.

֍

Upon a Midnight Clear

I would bet a brace of baubles plus a partridge in a pear tree that when Charles Dickens wrote *A Christmas Carol* no one wanted to identify with Scrooge, before he became converted to Christmas. How very different now. One is likely at this time of year to run into all kinds of people who view themselves as the Good Guys and who actually try to make you feel guilty if you celebrate Christmas. "It's become totally commercial," they virtuously say. "*We* don't have anything to do with it."

All I can reply, borrowing a word from Scrooge, is *Humbug*. Sure, okay, the stores may less-than-subtly put out their Christmas displays immediately after Halloween; the carols may be used to advertise fur coats or washing machines; the amount of phoniness surrounding Christmas in our culture may be astronomical. But Christmas itself remains untouched by all this crassness. It's still a matter of personal choice, and surely it's what happens in your own home that counts. In our house, Christmas has always been a very important time.

My background and heritage are strongly Christian, although I reserve the right to interpret things in my own way. In my interpretation, what Christmas celebrates is grace, a gift given from God to man, not because deserved, just because given. The birth of every wanted and loved child in this world is the same, a gift. The birth of *every* child should be this way. We're still frighteningly far from that, but maybe this festival can remind us. Christmas also reaches back to pre-Christian times—an ancient festival celebrating the winter solstice. *The Concise Oxford Dictionary* defines solstice very beautifully—"Either time (summer, winter) at which the sun is farthest from the equator and appears to pause before returning." For countless centuries in the northern lands, this time of year was a festival of faith, the faith that spring would return to the land. It links us with our ancestors a very long way back.

Christmas when I was a child was always a marvellous time. We used to go to the carol service on Christmas Eve, and those hymns still remain my favourites. "Hark the Herald Angels Sing," "Once in Royal David's City," and the one I loved best, "It Came Upon a Midnight Clear." It couldn't have been even near midnight when we walked home after those services, but it always seemed to me that I knew exactly what "midnight clear" meant. I had no sense then that there could be any kind of winter other than ours. It was a prairie town, and by Christmas the snow would always be thick and heavy, yet light and clean as well, something to be battled against and respected when it fell in blinding blizzards, but also something which created an upsurge of the heart at times such as those, walking back home on Christmas Eve with the carols still echoing in your head. The evening would be still, almost silent, and the air would be so dry and sharp you could practically touch the coldness. The snow would be dark-shadowed and then

suddenly it would look like sprinkled rainbows around
the sparse streetlights. Sometimes there were northern
lights. My memory, probably faulty, assigns the northern lights to *all* those Christmas eves, but they must
have appeared at least on some, a blazing eerie splendour across the sky, swift-moving, gigantic, like a
message. It was easy then to believe in the Word
made manifest. Not so easy now. And yet I can't
forget, ever, that the child, who was myself then,
experienced awe and recognized it.

We always had the ceremony of two Christmas
trees. One was in the late afternoon of Christmas Day,
and was at the home of my grandparents, my mother's
people, at the big brick house. There would be a
whole congregation of aunts and uncles and cousins
there on that day, and we would *have the tree* (that
is how we said it) before dinner. One of my aunts
was head of the nursing division in Saskatchewan's
public health department, and was a distinguished
professional woman. I didn't know that about her then.
What I knew was that each Christmas she came back
home with an astounding assortment of rare and wonderful things from what I felt must be the centre of
the great wide world, namely Regina. She used to
bring us those packages of Swiss cheese, each tiny piece
wrapped in silver paper, and decorations for the table
(a Santa with reindeer and sleigh, pine-cone men
painted iridescent white with red felt caps), and
chocolate Santas in red and gold paper, and chocolate
coins contained in heavy gold foil so that they looked
like my idea of Spanish doubloons and pieces of eight,
as in *Treasure Island*.

The dinner was enormous and exciting. We had
olives to begin with. We rarely had olives at any

other time, as they were expensive. My grandfather, of course, carved what was always known as The Bird, making the job into an impressive performance. He was never an eminently lovable man, but even he, with his stern ice-blue eyes, managed some degree of pleasantness at Christmas. The children at dinner were served last, which seems odd today. One of my memories is of myself at about six, sighing mightily as the plates were being passed to the adults and murmuring pathetically, "Couldn't I even have a crust?" My sense of drama was highly developed at a young age.

When the dishes were done—a mammoth task, washing all my grandmother's Limoges—we would make preparations to go home. I always had my own private foray into the kitchen then. I would go to the icebox (yes, icebox, with a block of ice delivered daily) and would tear off hunks of turkey, snatch a dozen or so olives, and wrap it all in wax paper. This was so I could have a small feast during the night, in case of sudden hunger, which invariably and improbably occurred each Christmas night.

The day of Christmas, however, began at home. The one I recall the best was the last Christmas we had with my father, for he died the next year. We were then living in my father's family home, a red-brick oddity with a rose window, a big dining room, a dozen nearly hidden cupboards and hidey-holes, and my father's study with the fireplace, above which hung a sinister bronze scimitar brought from India by an ancestor. I was nine that year, and my brother was two. The traditions in our family were strong. The children rose when they wakened (usually about 6 AM or earlier) and had their Christmas stockings. In those days, our stockings contained a Japanese orange at the toe, some red-and-white peppermint canes, a bunch of unshelled peanuts, and one or two small presents—a kaleidoscope or a puzzle consisting of two or three interlocked pieces of metal which you had to try to prise apart, and never could.

As my memory tells it to me, my very young brother and myself had our Christmas stockings in our parents' bedroom, and Christmas had officially begun. We were then sent back to bed until the decent hour of 7:30 or 8:00 AM, at which time I could get dressed in my sweater and my plaid skirt with the straps over the shoulder, while my mother dressed my brother in his sweater and infant overalls. We then went down for breakfast. In our house, you always had breakfast before you had The Tree. This wasn't such a bad thing. Christmas breakfast was sausage rolls, which we never had for breakfast any other time. These had been made weeks before, and frozen in the unheated summer kitchen. We had frozen food years before it became commercially viable. I guess our only amazement about it when it came on the market was that they could do it in summer as well. After breakfast, we all went into the study, where we had to listen to the Empire Broadcast on the radio, a report from all those pink-colored areas on the world map, culminating in the King's speech. The voices seemed to go on forever. I don't recall how my brother was kept pacified—with candy, probably— but I recall myself fidgeting. This was the ritual—the Empire Broadcast *before* The Tree, a practice which now seems to me to have been slightly bizarre, and yet probably was not so. Our parents wanted to hear it, and in those days it wasn't going to be repeated in capsule form on the late night news. I guess it also taught us that you could wait for what you wanted —but that's a concept about which I've always felt pretty ambiguous.

At last, at last, we could go into The Living Room for The Tree. The Living Room, I should say, was the only formal room in that house. We did not live in it; it was totally misnamed. It was For Best. It was the room in which my mother gave the afternoon teas which were then required of people like the wives of lawyers in towns like ours. The Living Room had a lot of stiff upholstered furniture, always just so. It was, as well, chilly. But it was the place for The Tree, and it seemed somehow the right place, something special.

And there it was, The Tree. *Oh.*

I could see now why we'd been so carefully kept out of the room until this moment. There, beside The Tree, were our presents. For my brother, a rocking horse, two horses cut out of wood and painted white with green flecks, joined by a seat between them. Our dad had made it, for he was a very good amateur carpenter. And for me—wow! A desk. A small desk, found in an attic, as I later learned, and painted by our dad, a bright blue with flower patterns, a desk which opened up and had your own private cubbyholes in it. My own desk. My first. That remains the nicest present that anyone ever gave me, the present from my parents when I was nine.

It was only many years later that I realized that the rocking horse and the desk had been our presents then because no one could afford to buy anything much in that depression and drought year of 1935. And it wasn't until long afterwards, either, that I realized how lucky and relatively unscathed we'd been, and how many people in this country that year must have had virtually no Christmas at all.

One other aspect of my childhood Christmases was Lee Ling. He was the man who ran our town's Chinese restaurant, and he lived without his family for all the time he was there. In those days, Chinese wives were scarcely allowed into this country at all. My father did Lee's legal work, and every Christmas Lee gave us a turkey, a large box of chocolates, and a box of lichee nuts. You might possibly say that Lee did it because he hoped to get on the right side of the lawyer. My father wasn't like that, and neither was Lee. The point of this story, however, is that Lee Ling continued at Christmas to give our family a turkey, a box of chocolates and a box of lichee nuts after my father died, for years, until Lee himself died. To me, that says something valuable about both Lee Ling and my father.

Much later on, when my own children were young and growing up, our Christmases became patterns which reflected my own Christmases many years ago, but with our own additions. We had ten Christmases in our house in England, Elm Cottage, before my children became adults and I moved back home to Canada to stay. Christmas in that house was always something very good and warm, and there were usually a lot of young Canadian visitors there with us at that time.

As in my childhood, the Christmas stockings were opened early in the morning. The difference was, with us, that my kids always made a Christmas stocking for me as well, their own idea. The stockings had candies, including the same kind of chocolate coins, but they also had a variety of joke presents, sometimes kids' books when my kids were no longer children, because we've always liked good children's books and we frequently give them to one another.

Some of the traditions continued. In our house, you always have breakfast before you have The Tree. But in our time, The Tree was in my study, not a "special" place, and we frequently went in wearing housecoats and dressing-gowns and bearing large mugs of coffee. The presents were distributed one at a time so everyone could look at each. We made it last about two hours. I don't think gifts need to be meaningless. I love opening presents from people who care about me, and I love giving presents to people I care about, hoping I've chosen something they will really like, something that fits their own personality, something that will be a symbol of my feeling for them.

Our dinner at Elm Cottage was always fairly hectic. I was in charge of what we called The Bird, as it had been called in my own childhood. I twittered and worried over that turkey, wondering if I had put it in the oven soon enough, or if I was going to overcook it to the point of total disaster. It always turned out fine, an amazing fact when one considers that our stove was so small as to be almost ridiculous and that even cramming a 15-pound turkey into it at all was a major task. The turkey, I modestly admit, was accompanied by some of the best sage-and-onion stuffing in the entire world. Our friend Alice always made her super cranberry sauce, which included walnuts and orange, and was the best I've ever tasted. Our friend Sandy always used to do the plum pudding, which she cleverly heated on a small electric burner set up in the hall, as there wasn't room on the stove. My daughter had been the one to organize the cake, a month before, and everyone had given it a stir for luck. It was a very co-operative meal. Yes, the women did prepare all the food. But the men carved The Bird, served the dinner, and did the dishes. It always seemed to me that our efforts meshed pretty well. Our friend Peter once said that Elm Cottage was a scene of "agreeable anarchy." I think it was, and that phrase certainly describes our Christmas dinners, at which we never had less than a dozen people, and sometimes more.

After dinner, we would move to The Music Room, which was our version of The Living Room, except that we really lived in it. It had a good stereo and a feeling that people could come in and sit around the fireplace and play their guitars and sing their own songs. This used to happen a lot, and always at Christmas. We made new traditions. One of my own favourites was a ritual which said that at some point in the evening, our friend Ian would play and sing two songs for me. Corny and out-of-date they may be, but I like them. They were "She Walks These Hills in a Long Black Veil" and "St. James Infirmary Blues."

Those Christmases at Elm Cottage had a feeling of real community. For me, this is what this festival is all about—the sense of God's grace, and the sense of our own family and extended family, the sense of human community.

In 1967, Al Purdy was getting together a collection by Canadian writers on the theme of our views of America. Taking time out from writing his own poetry, sighing and swearing and smoking his innumerable cigars, Purdy was conning or charming a lot of Canadian writers into contributing. What it turned out to be, in the end, was an extremely interesting and diverse collection of essays and poems, published in 1968 under the title of *The New Romans*.

Open Letter to the Mother of Joe Bass

I don't know what you look like. We will not meet. I don't know how old you are. About my age, I would guess, which is forty-one. I don't know how many kids you have. I have two. My daughter is fifteen, and my son is twelve. You have a twelve-year-old son also.

My son was born in Ghana, and there was no doctor present. The doctor was overworked, and I was okay and normal, so there was only a midwife in attendance. She was a Ghanaian matriarch, four kids of her own, and no male doctor could have known what she knew.

"It will be a boy," she promised to me as the hours passed by. "Only a man could be so stubborn."

When I was in pain, she put out her hands to me and let me clench them, and I held to those hands as though they were my hope of life.

"It will be soon over," she said. "Would I lie to you? Look, I know. I have borne."

She did know. I had no anaesthetic, and when she

222

delivered him, she laid him, damp and thin and blood-smeared, across my belly.

"There," she said. "What did I tell you? Your boy, he is here."

She was the only other person present when I looked over God's shoulder at the birth of my son. She had had her children too, and she knew what it was that was happening. She knew that it had to be felt in the flesh to be really known.

In twelve years so far, touch wood, my son has been lucky. Once in Africa he had malaria, and a few other times, in Canada and England, he had such things as throat infections or chicken pox. Each time I have been afraid in that one way, guts-of-ice feeling that I could probably face anything at all except that something really bad should happen to one of my kids.

Now he rides on his bike for countless miles around the countryside. He is a science man at heart, and his electric train set has complicated switches and intricate wiring which he has rigged up himself and which miraculously work and make the miniature engines do as he bids. He has lived life so far among people who were basically friendly towards him. That is not to say that he has never felt pain. He has. More, even, than I know, and I know some of it. But at least until this point in his life, his pain has been something which he could, in some way, deal with by himself.

I have seen your son only once, Mrs. Bass. That was in a newspaper photograph. In Detroit, he went out one evening when his playmates asked him to. It was not an evening to be out. Your son was shot by the police. By accident, the paper said. Shot by accident in the neck. The police were aiming at Billy Furr, who was walking out of Mack Liquors, not with a fortune in his hands but with precisely six tins of stolen beer. When Billy Furr saw the police, something told him to run and keep on running, so he did that, and he was shot dead. But the police had fired more than once, and Joe Bass happened to be in the way. The papers did not say whether he was expected to recover or not, nor how much a twelve-year-old could recover from something like that. A Negro twelve-year-old.

Your son looked a skinny kid, a little taller than my twelve-year-old but not as robust. He was lying on the sidewalk, and his eyes were open. He was seeing everything, I guess, including himself. He was bleeding, and one of his hands lay languidly outstretched in a spillage of blood. His face didn't have any expression at all. I looked at the picture for quite a long time. Then I put it away, but it would not be put away. The blank kid-face there kept fluctuating in my mind. Sometimes it was the face of your son, sometimes of mine.

Then I recalled another newspaper photograph. It was of a North Vietnamese woman. Some marvellous new kind of napalm had just come into use. I do not understand the technicalities. This substance, when it alights, flaming, onto skin, cannot be removed. It adheres. The woman was holding a child who looked about eighteen months old, and she was trying to pluck something away from the burn-blackening area of the child's face. I wondered how she felt when her child newly took on life and emerged, and if she had almost imagined she was looking over God's shoulder then.

Mrs. Bass, these are the two pictures. I know they

are not fair. I know the many-sidedness of that country in which you live. I know the people I love there, who are more heartbroken than I at the descent into lunacy. Also, I am a North American—I cannot exclude myself from the dilemma. I cannot say *them*. It is forced upon me to say *us*. Perhaps you know who the enemy is—and perhaps it is I.

Once, a long time ago, from the eyes of twenty, I wrote a poem about my father, or maybe about the local cemetery, in which the words said, "Under the stone lies my father, ten years dead, who would never know as his this bastard world he sired." It did not occur to me then that I would one day stand in that same relation to the world—no longer as a child, but as a parent.

I am not even sure who is responsible. Responsibility seems to have become too diffuse, and a whole continent (if not, indeed, a whole world) appears to be spinning in automation. The wheels turn, but no one admits to turning them. People with actual names and places of belonging are killed, and there is increasingly little difference between these acts and the fake deaths of the cowboys who never were. The fantasy is taking over, like the strangler vines of the jungle taking over the trees. It is all happening on TV.

Except that it isn't. You know, because you felt the pain in your own flesh, that evening when the police shot your son. Is it necessary to feel pain in our own flesh before we really know? More and more, I think that it probably is.

I have spent fifteen years of my life writing novels and other things. I have had, if any faith at all, a faith in the word. *In the beginning was the Word, and the Word was with God, and the Word was God.* The kind of belief that many writers have—the belief that if we are to make ourselves known to one another, if we are really to know the reality of another, we must communicate with what is almost the only means we have—human speech. There are other means of communication, I know, but they are limited because they are so personal and individual. We can make love; we can hold and comfort our children. Otherwise, we are stuck with words. We have to try to talk to one another, because this imperfect means is the only one we have.

And yet—I look at the picture of your twelve-year-old son on the sidewalks of Detroit, pillowed in blood. And I wonder—if it were in physical fact *my* son, of the same age, would I be able to go on writing novels, in the belief that this was a worthwhile thing to be doing in this year (as they say) of our Lord? Mrs. Bass, I do not think I can answer that question.

I am afraid for all our children.

The whole tragic area of Canadian history which encompasses the struggles, against great odds, of the prairie Indian and Métis peoples in the 1800's is one which has long concerned and troubled me. This article has a great deal of relevance to my own life-view, a relevance which is to be found in much of my work, but perhaps seen in its broadest sense in my novel, *The Diviners*, and more narrowly and politically (as a study of another nomadic tribal society in conflict with an imperialist power) in "The Poem and the Spear" in this collection. The following article was published in 1975 in somewhat shorter form. I am pleased to have the opportunity of republishing it now, as a tribute both to Gabriel Dumont and to George Woodcock, another great man of our people, a man to whom we owe so much.

Man of Our People

For years I have been hoping that someone would write a biography of Gabriel Dumont. When I began learning more about the history of our West than the pitifully small amount I learned in school, Louis Riel seemed the most compelling man in the prairie past, and yet as I read more about the Métis people and the North-West Rebellion of 1885, it seemed to me that Dumont was fully as interesting and significant, a truly heroic man. The enigma of the relationship between these two totally different men—Riel, the dreamer, the prophet, the spiritual leader, and Dumont, the huntsman, the man of action, the military leader—has always posed the question *Why?* Why did Gabriel obey Riel so unswervingly, right to the end, when he knew that Riel was vacillating and that Riel's military tactics were virtually non-existent? That whole relationship and the tragic story of the last stand of the Métis has haunted me. Many Canadians must have felt the same.

When I learned that George Woodcock was writing a book on Gabriel Dumont, I rejoiced, because it seemed to me that if anyone could do justice to the subject, that person was Woodcock. His broad grasp of history, his deep sympathy with oppressed peoples everywhere, his keenly critical eye and analytical mind, his frequently brilliant writing style, and, yes, the sheer wisdom of the man—all these made him the right person to write a powerful and definitive book on Gabriel Dumont. And he has done so. *The Métis Chief and his Lost World* is one of the strongest and most moving books I have read in a long time.

Riel, in Woodcock's view, is the one who has been remembered and written about more than Dumont, because as a people we tend to identify with martyrs. Be that as it may (and I think it is at least an arguable point), Dumont is undoubtedly, as Woodcock puts it, "a hero in the high romantic vein," and Canadians do, I agree, "suspect the sheer gigantic irrationalism of the heroic, for we like to consider ourselves a reasonable people."

In the 1885 uprising, Dumont favoured the old Métis method of warfare—a method which, incidentally, has been used by every tribal society that I know about—namely a guerrilla warfare of sharp attack and quick withdrawal, preferably on very familiar terrain. It is a sound method, but one which, when faced not with a force possessing superior qualities of courage but with a force possessing vastly superior weapons, is almost bound to fail. The Métis in 1885, faced with the Canadian volunteer army, with the North-West Mounted Police contingents, with Middleton's cannon, and with the recently invented Gatling gun, could not have held out indefinitely, as Gabriel must have realized. There are, however, degrees of failure, and in the last stand what the Métis might have achieved was bargaining power. If Gabriel Dumont had been given his head throughout the '85 campaigns, and especially at Batoche, the Métis would certainly not have lost so disastrously; they would have been at least in a position, as Woodcock says, "that would make concessions inevitable." The same was true at the battle of Culloden in 1746, when the clansmen were literally mowed down by the British cannon, while Prince Charlie dithered and would not give the order to fire, until the clans finally charged insanely and were slaughtered and the Highland social order totally broken, with nothing negotiable. Indeed, Woodcock comments on the irony of the fact that Sir John A. Macdonald, persistently deaf to the needs and pleas of the Métis, "belonged by ancestry to the clans that at Culloden stood in defense of a primitive culture against a complex civilization, in the same way as Gabriel Dumont and his people were preparing to stand on the Saskatchewan."

It was the first war that Canada fought without assistance from British troops, although the dreadful General Middleton was a British import. It has always seemed ironic to me that this war so much resembled the colonialist-imperialist wars of Britain, from whom Canada had recently become independent. Perhaps I am making too much of this parallel, although I think it truly exists. Woodcock believes, and of course he is perfectly right, that the crucial battle in 1885 was between those who "lived in and on and with the environment—whether they were Indians or Métis— and those who wished to live off it, to dominate and exploit it."

Who was this plainsman whose life had such enormous impact upon our history? Gabriel Dumont was born in the Red River settlement in 1837, into a family of fine and even flamboyant hunters who had come originally from the Saskatchewan territory. In the early 1800's, the Métis from further west tended to move towards the Red River, where they were hired by the North-West Company, and where they joined the local Métis in the great buffalo hunts. Woodcock is especially good in describing the history of the Métis, half-French and half-Indian people, and the events which would make the Rebellion of 1870 an inevitability. The Dumonts, however, did not remain at Red River. They returned to the Saskatchewan Valley, where Gabriel spent much of his boyhood around Fort Pitt. He had no formal education and remained illiterate all his life, but he became probably the best of the buffalo hunters, and he ultimately learned six Indian languages. On another trek back to Red River, Gabriel at the age of ten received his first gun, which he called Le Petit, the name he gave to all his other rifles from that time on. He fought in his first battle (against a camp of Sioux in a hunting dispute) when he was thirteen.

There are many legends about Gabriel in young manhood, some no doubt wild exaggerations. Some of the more reliable tales were told by Gabriel himself as an old man, and these, Woodcock says, "project . . . a personality nearer to Homer than to Hollywood." In 1858, Gabriel married Madeleine Wilkie, and for some time moved back and forth from the Saskatchewan to Red River to trade buffalo meat and hides for Hudson's Bay Company goods. The Company was exploitive, and like many Métis, Gabriel was constantly in debt to them at this point in his life. In 1863, he became the leader of the Saskatchewan hunt, at the age of twenty-five, and remained the chief of the Saskatchewan Métis from that time on.

When the Manitoba Métis, fearing to lose their land, appointed Louis Riel as their leader, and when events moved towards the uprising of 1870, there is evidence to believe that Dumont went to Fort Garry to offer Riel his support, which was apparently not accepted, or was felt not to be needed, as such support would have been military, Métis hunters plus Indian allies, and, as Woodcock says, "Riel developed desperate policies that could succeed only by means of violence, and yet he shrank from violence when it came." After 1870, when Riel was in exile in Montana, many of the Red River Métis moved west, following the decreasing buffalo herds and also because of a sense of betrayal by the Canadian government. Fifteen years later, many of them would stand with Dumont and his men.

Dumont staked out a claim to his land in 1872, and did some farming, although basically he remained a hunter. He also began a ferry at a place still known as "Gabriel's Crossing." Woodcock says that even today, "nowhere in the triangle between Saskatoon, Prince Albert and Battleford is it necessary to add the surname of Dumont when talking of him."

The events leading up to 1885 make sad reading, indeed. The buffalo were disappearing, owing to wasteful hunting and to the slaughter on the part of American commercial hunters when the herds were on that side of the border. More settlers were coming in, and the Métis were understandably concerned about their title to their lands. In 1873, a council was established, of which Gabriel was elected chief, and a constitution drawn up, a practical set of laws which suited the loosely bound freedom-oriented social organization of the Métis villages. It is, incidentally, the flexible, practical nature of Métis society which attracts Woodcock, and he describes it as having been, for a time, similar to a well-working anarchical society. As he is probably the world's greatest authority on anarchy as a social system, this gives us fascinating insights, both into the social structure of the Métis and into one of Woodcock's many qualifications for writing this book. At this stage, all that Gabriel and his people wanted was government protection of the Métis lands and their ancient rights of hunting, trapping, and fishing. We watch with dismay the situation worsening—the constant appeals of the Métis to Ottawa; Sir John A. Macdonald's determination to get the railway through, but his absolute refusal to deal with the problems of the Métis or even to admit that the people of the north-west prairies *had* any problems; the way in which men like Archbishop Taché and Lieutenant-Governor Morris, at Red River, tried to get Ottawa to listen, without success, although a few men like the Deputy Minister of the Interior, Colonel J. S. Dennis, did make serious attempts to get Macdonald to attend to the problem justly. When finally

the government did send a representative to enquire
into the land claims in Saskatchewan, he spoke no
French and left the Métis claims totally neglected.
The Indians were signing treaties throughout this
period (with notable and honourable exceptions such
as Big Bear), and had their reservations and hand-outs,
pathetically inadequate and criminally exploitive
though the treaties were. Under the Canadian government, the Métis had no legal title to any lands at all.

When Gabriel Dumont and a few other men rode
to Montana in 1884 to ask Louis Riel to return, it was
at this stage only with the thought of obtaining Riel's
advice. Riel was experienced and educated. Perhaps
he could get the ear of the Canadian government. But
he, too, failed in this direction, after months of meet-
ings and unanswered petitions to Ottawa. Events
moved inexorably towards insurrection.

The events of 1885 are well known, but Woodcock
describes them so dramatically and movingly that it
is almost a new experience to read of them here. The
withdrawal of the priests' support; the Métis victory
at Duck Lake; the alliance with the Indians; the press-
ing through of steel by the CPR; the raising of the
brave naive young volunteer forces in Canada; the
indecisive and hard-won Métis victory at Fish Creek;
the final tragedy at Batoche. We are not shown the
Indians' uprising in great detail, for, as Woodcock
points out, the two rebellions went on virtually sepa-
rately. The best reconstruction of the Indians' side of
the uprising is to be found, in my opinion, in Rudy
Wiebe's fine historical novel, *The Temptations of Big
Bear*.

All the way through, we see the centrality of

Dumont, who, having committed himself to battle, was prepared to go through with it, and we see Riel, torn with himself, hating bloodshed, fatally hesitating, trying to believe a miracle would happen. Woodcock quotes some fascinating parts of Dumont's own account of Batoche, dictated a few years later. Then it was over, with Riel destined for the scaffold, and Dumont to a life of temporary exile in the u.s.a., trying to raise support for a cause which was lost, and finally granted amnesty and going back home to die. The great days of the prairie horselords were over, and when the Métis voices would ultimately be heard again, it would be within a different context, a different world from the world of Gabriel Dumont.

As to *why* Gabriel Dumont went along with Riel's commands when he knew them to be a military disaster, in some ways that question will always remain an enigma, and perhaps it is right that it should. But Woodcock's analysis of the friendship and loyalty between the two men is the most convincing and complete that I have ever read, and his conjectures seem to me to be totally valid. Dumont emerges as a man of great strength, spiritual as well as physical, a man who remained true to the code of honour of his people, a man who chose (rightly, I believe, in his case, although this would not have been true in Riel's) to live rather than to die as a martyr. As Woodcock says, speaking of Dumont as a young man, "There would be times when Gabriel Dumont acted brutally; never times when he acted meanly." He could, and did, for a short time in his exile, join Buffalo Bill Cody's circus—and such a travesty did not diminish him. He was not a man of words, like Riel, but he was no less complex a person.

Dumont composed a prayer when riding back to Saskatchewan from Montana, in 1884, with Riel, a prayer which he thereafter repeated every day for the rest of his life:

Lord, strengthen my courage, my faith and my honour, that I may profit all my life from the blessing I have received in Thy Holy Name.

Courage, faith and honour. Dumont certainly had all these. And something else.

A recent poem of George Woodcock's is entitled *On Completing a Life of Gabriel Dumont*. The last lines are these:

But what is the echo I hear compellingly ring
In my ear as you bow sardonically into your defile
Of dark death? What does it tell me I share with you?
Is it, fierce stranger, that freedom is a word our hearts
  both sing?

Has the voice of Gabriel anything to tell us here and now, in a world totally different from his? I believe it has. The spirits of Dumont and Riel, of Big Bear and Poundmaker, after the long silence, are speaking once again through their people, their descendants. Will we ever reach a point when it is no longer necessary to say Them and Us? I believe we must reach that point, or perish. Canadians who, like myself, are the descendants of various settlers, many of whom came to this country as oppressed or dispossessed peoples, must hear native peoples' voices and ultimately become part of them, for they speak not only of the soul-searing injustices done to them but also of their rediscovered sense of self-worth and their ability to tell and teach the things needed to be known. We have a consumer-oriented society, and one which is still in many ways colonialist, because still other-dominated, now by America, a neo-colonialist power whose real and individual people (as distinct from governments or corporations) are our spiritual and blood relations, a fact which must never be forgotten, for we need one another. We have largely forgotten how to live with, protect, and pay homage to our earth and the other creatures who share it with us—as witness the killing of rivers and lakes; the killing of the whales; the proliferation of apartment blocks on irreplaceable farmlands. We have so much to learn and act upon, and time is getting short. Those other societies which existed before imperialism, industrialism, mass exploitation, and commercial greed were certainly far from ideal, nor can we return to them, but they knew about living in relationship to the land, and they may ultimately be the societies from whose values we must try to learn.

There are many ways in which those of us who are not Indian or Métis have not yet earned the right to call Gabriel Dumont ancestor. But I do so, all the same. His life, his legend, and his times are a part of our past which we desperately need to understand and pay heed to.

I wrote this article in 1971, when I was beginning my novel *The Diviners*. I see now that I used it as one more means of working out a theme that appears in the novel, that is, the question of where one belongs and why, and the meaning to oneself of the ancestors, both the long-ago ones and those in remembered history. Until I re-read these articles, I didn't realize I had written so much on this theme before I ever dealt with it fictionally. I didn't realize, either, how compulsively I'd written about the river, the same river that appears in the novel.

§§

Where the World Began

A strange place it was, that place where the world began. A place of incredible happenings, splendours and revelations, despairs like multitudinous pits of isolated hells. A place of shadow-spookiness, inhabited by the unknowable dead. A place of jubilation and of mourning, horrible and beautiful.

It was, in fact, a small prairie town.

Because that settlement and that land were my first and for many years my only real knowledge of this planet, in some profound way they remain my world, my way of viewing. My eyes were formed there. Towns like ours, set in a sea of land, have been described thousands of times as dull, bleak, flat, uninteresting. I have had it said to me that the railway trip across Canada is spectacular, except for the prairies, when it would be desirable to go to sleep for several days, until the ordeal is over. I am always unable to argue this point effectively. All I can say is—

well, you really have to live there to know that country. The town of my childhood could be called bizarre, agonizingly repressive or cruel at times, and the land in which it grew could be called harsh in the violence of its seasonal changes. But never merely flat or uninteresting. Never dull.

In winter, we used to hitch rides on the back of the milk sleigh, our moccasins squeaking and slithering on the hard rutted snow of the roads, our hands in ice-bubbled mitts hanging onto the box edge of the sleigh for dear life, while Bert grinned at us through his great frosted moustache and shouted the horse into speed, daring us to stay put. Those mornings, rising, there would be the perpetual fascination of the frost feathers on windows, the ferns and flowers and eerie faces traced there during the night by unseen artists of the wind. Evenings, coming back from skating, the sky would be black but not dark, for you could see a cold glitter of stars from one side of the earth's rim to the other. And then the sometime astonishment when you saw the Northern Lights flaring across the sky, like the scrawled signature of God. After a blizzard, when the snowploughs hadn't yet got through, school would be closed for the day, the assumption being that the town's young could not possibly flounder through five feet of snow in the pursuit of education. We would then gaily don snowshoes and flounder for miles out into the white dazzling deserts, in pursuit of a different kind of knowing. If you came back too close to night, through the woods at the foot of the town hill, the thin black branches of poplar and chokecherry now meringued with frost, sometimes you heard coyotes. Or maybe the banshee wolf-voices were really only inside your head.

Summers were scorching, and when no rain came and the wheat became bleached and dried before it headed, the faces of farmers and townsfolk would not smile much, and you took for granted, because it never seemed to have been any different, the frequent knocking at the back door and the young men standing there, mumbling or thrusting defiantly their requests for a drink of water and a sandwich if you could spare it. They were riding the freights, and you never knew where they had come from, or where they might end up, if anywhere. The Drought and Depression were like evil deities which had been there always. You understood and did not understand.

Yet the outside world had its continuing marvels. The poplar bluffs and the small river were filled and surrounded with a zillion different grasses, stones, and weed flowers. The meadowlarks sang undaunted from the twanging telephone wires along the gravel highway. Once we found an old flat-bottomed scow, and launched her, poling along the shallow brown waters, mending her with wodges of hastily chewed Spearmint, grounding her among the tangles of yellow marsh marigolds that grew succulently along the banks of the shrunken river, while the sun made our skins smell dusty-warm.

My best friend lived in an apartment above some stores on Main Street (its real name was Mountain Avenue, goodness knows why), an elegant apartment with royal-blue velvet curtains. The back roof, scarcely sloping at all, was corrugated tin, of a furnace-like warmth on a July afternoon, and we would sit there drinking lemonade and looking across the back lane at the Fire Hall. Sometimes our vigil would be rewarded. Oh joy! Somebody's house burning down!

We had an almost-perfect callousness in some ways. Then the wooden tower's bronze bell would clonk and toll like a thousand speeded funerals in a time of plague, and in a few minutes the team of giant black horses would cannon forth, pulling the fire wagon like some scarlet chariot of the Goths, while the firemen clung with one hand, adjusting their helmets as they went.

The oddities of the place were endless. An elderly lady used to serve, as her afternoon tea offering to other ladies, soda biscuits spread with peanut butter and topped with a whole marshmallow. Some considered this slightly eccentric, when compared with chopped egg sandwiches, and admittedly talked about her behind her back, but no one ever refused these delicacies or indicated to her that they thought she had slipped a cog. Another lady dyed her hair a bright and cheery orange, by strangers often mistaken at twenty paces for a feather hat. My own beloved stepmother wore a silver fox neckpiece, a whole pelt, *with the embalmed (?) head still on.* My Ontario Irish grandfather said "sparrow grass," a more interesting term than asparagus. The town dump was known as "the nuisance grounds," a phrase fraught with weird connotations, as though the effluvia of our lives was beneath contempt but at the same time was subtly threatening to the determined and sometimes hysterical propriety of our ways.

Some oddities were, as idiom had it, "funny ha ha"; others were "funny peculiar." Some were not so very funny at all. An old man lived, deranged, in a shack in the valley. Perhaps he wasn't even all that old, but to us he seemed a wild Methuselah figure, shambling among the underbrush and the tall couchgrass, muttering indecipherable curses of blessings, a prophet who had forgotten his prophesies. Everyone in town knew him, but no one knew him. He lived among us as though only occasionally and momentarily visible. The kids called him Andy Gump, and feared him. Some sought to prove their bravery by tormenting him. They were the mediaeval bear baiters, and he the lumbering bewildered bear, half blind, only rarely turning to snarl. Everything is to be found in a town like mine. Belsen, writ small but with the same ink.

All of us cast stones in one shape or another. In grade school, among the vulnerable and violet girls we were, the feared and despised were those few older girls from what was charmingly termed "the wrong side of the tracks." Tough in talk and tougher in muscle, they were said to be whores already. And may have been, that being about the only profession readily available to them.

The dead lived in that place, too. Not only the grandparents who had, in local parlance, "passed on" and who gloomed, bearded or bonneted, from the sepia photographs in old albums, but also the uncles, forever eighteen or nineteen, whose names were carved on the granite family stones in the cemetery, but whose bones lay in France. My own young mother lay in that graveyard, beside other dead of our kin, and when I was ten, my father, too, only forty, left the living town for the dead dwelling on the hill.

When I was eighteen, I couldn't wait to get out of that town, away from the prairies. I did not know then that I would carry the land and town all my life within my skull, that they would form the mainspring and source of the writing I was to do, wherever and however far away I might live.

This was my territory in the time of my youth, and in a sense my life since then has been an attempt to look at it, to come to terms with it. Stultifying to the mind it certainly could be, and sometimes was, but not to the imagination. It was many things, but it was never dull.

The same, I now see, could be said for Canada in general. Why on earth did generations of Canadians pretend to believe this country dull? We knew perfectly well it wasn't. Yet for so long we did not proclaim what we knew. If our upsurge of so-called nationalism seems odd or irrelevant to outsiders, and even to some of our own people (*what's all the fuss about?*), they might try to understand that for many years we valued ourselves insufficiently, living as we did under the huge shadows of those two dominating figures, Uncle Sam and Britannia. We have only just begun to value ourselves, our land, our abilities. We have only just begun to recognize our legends and to give shape to our myths.

There are, God knows, enough aspects to deplore about this country. When I see the killing of our lakes and rivers with industrial wastes, I feel rage and despair. When I see our industries and natural resources increasingly taken over by America, I feel an overwhelming discouragement, especially as I cannot simply say "damn Yankees." It should never be forgotten that it is we ourselves who have sold such a large amount of our birthright for a mess of plastic Progress. When I saw the War Measures Act being invoked in 1970, I lost forever the vestigial remains of the naive wish-belief that repression could not happen here, or would not. And yet, of course, I had known all along in the deepest and often hidden caves of the heart that anything can happen anywhere, for the seeds of both man's freedom and his captivity are found everywhere, even in the microcosm of a prairie town. But in raging against our injustices, our stupidities, I do so *as family*, as I did, and still do in writing, about those aspects of my town which I hated and which are always in some ways aspects of myself.

The land still draws me more than other lands. I have lived in Africa and in England, but splendid as both can be, they do not have the power to move me in the same way as, for example, that part of southern Ontario where I spent four months last summer in a cedar cabin beside a river. "Scratch a Canadian, and you find a phony pioneer," I used to say to myself in warning. But all the same it is true, I think, that we are not yet totally alienated from physical earth, and let us only pray we do not become so. I once thought that my lifelong fear and mistrust of cities made me a kind of old-fashioned freak; now I see it differently.

The cabin has a long window across its front western wall, and sitting at the oak table there in the mornings, I used to look out at the river and at the tall trees beyond, green-gold in the early light. The river was bronze; the sun caught it strangely, reflecting upon its surface the near-shore sand ripples underneath. Suddenly, the crescenting of a fish, gone before the eye could clearly give image to it. The old man next door said these leaping fish were carp. Himself, he preferred muskie, for he was a real fisherman and the muskie gave him a fight. The wind most often blew from the south, and the river flowed toward the south, so when the water was wind-riffled, and the current was strong, the river seemed to be flowing both ways. I liked this, and interpreted it as an omen, a natural symbol.

A few years ago, when I was back in Winnipeg, I gave a talk at my old college. It was open to the public, and afterward a very old man came up to me and asked me if my maiden name had been Wemyss. I said yes, thinking he might have known my father or my grandfather. But no. "When I was a young lad," he said, "I once worked for your great-grandfather, Robert Wemyss, when he had the sheep ranch at Raeburn." I think that was a moment when I realized all over again something of great importance to me. My long-ago families came from Scotland and Ireland, but in a sense that no longer mattered so much. My true roots were here.

I am not very patriotic, in the usual meaning of that word. I cannot say "My country right or wrong" in any political, social or literary context. But one thing is inalterable, for better or worse, for life.

This is where my world began. A world which includes the ancestors—both my own and other people's ancestors who become mine. A world which formed me, and continues to do so, even while I fought it in some of its aspects, and continue to do so. A world which gave me my own lifework to do, because it was here that I learned the sight of my own particular eyes.

Acknowledgements

*The following articles have been published, some in slightly
different form, in these publications:*

A Place to Stand On—Mosaic, April 1970

Sayonara, Agamemnon—Holiday, January 1966

The Epic Love of Elmii Bonderii—Holiday, November
1965

The Very Best Intentions—Holiday, November 1964

The Wild Blue Yonder—Vancouver Sun, September 1,
1973

Put Out One or Two More Flags—Vancouver Sun, February 5, 1972

Road from the Isles—Maclean's, May 2, 1966

Down East—Vancouver Sun, March 20, 1971

Inside the Idiot Box—Vancouver Sun, June 17, 1972

I Am a Taxi—Vancouver Sun, February 7, 1970

Living Dangerously by Mail—Vancouver Sun, September
23, 1972

The Shack—Weekend Magazine, May 11, 1974

Upon a Midnight Clear—Weekend Magazine, December
21, 1974

Open Letter to the Mother of Joe Bass—*The New
Romans*—Hurtig, 1968—reprinted Maclean's, October
1968

Man of Our People—Canadian Forum, December–January
1976

Where the World Began—Maclean's, December 1972

ABOUT THE AUTHOR

MARGARET LAURENCE was born in 1926 in Neepawa, a small town in Manitoba and was educated at the University of Manitoba. Her literary output includes six novels, critiques, commentaries, children's literature and short stories. In 1960 her novel *This Side Jordan* was published in the United States, England and Canada and won for her Canada's Beta Sigma Phi Award for the best novel by a Canadian. Following this were *The Prophet's Camel Bell*, a book about Somaliland, *The Tomorrow-Tamer*, a collection of short stories and *The Stone Angel*, a novel. In 1967, her novel *A Jest of God* won the Governor General's Award; it later became the basis for the film *Rachel, Rachel*. *The Fire-Dwellers* (1969) was followed by a collection of short stories, *A Bird in the House* (1970). Her other works include *Jason's Quest*, a children's story, *Long Drums and Cannons*, a study of Nigerian literature and *The Diviners*, which won the 1974 Governor General's Award.

During 1969–70, Margaret Laurence was Writer-in-Residence at the University of Toronto. She subsequently held the same post at the University of Western Ontario and Trent University. She has lived in England, Somaliland and Ghana and now makes her home in Lakefield, Ontario.

SEAL BOOKS

Offers you a list of outstanding fiction, non-fiction and classics of Canadian literature in paperback by Canadian authors, available at all good bookstores throughout Canada.

The Mark of Canadian Bestsellers

THE MANAWAKA SERIES

by

Margaret Laurence,

Canada's most celebrated novelist,
Winner of the Governor-General's
Award

The Manawaka stories, set in the most famous fictional town in Canada, offer a clear-eyed vision of Canadian land and people.

This skilled story teller balances humor and pathos as she portrays the human condition through characters struggling to come to terms with themselves and with the world.

THE STONE ANGEL
A JEST OF GOD
THE FIRE-DWELLERS
A BIRD IN THE HOUSE
THE DIVINERS

Seal Books

Available in paperback at all good bookstores
across Canada.

MSML-1